MW00625348

Confess Unhappy Housewife

How I changed my bullsh*t stories to create a life I love

Kirstin Smith

Confessions of an Unhappy Housewife

How I Changed My Bullsh*t Stories to Create a Life I Love

All Rights Reserved

COPYRIGHT © 2022 Kirstin Smith

This book may not be reproduced, transmitted, or stored in whole or in part by any means, including graphic, electronic, or mechanical, without the express written consent of the publisher except in the case of brief questions embodied in critical articles and reviews.

ISBN: 978-0-578-38838-0

Cover design by Sooraj Mathew

Edited by Hilary Jastram

To all the moms desperate to fill their empty cup,
this book is for you.

TABLE OF CONTENTS

PREFACE

These pages contain the story of my journey: how I went from an aspiring PhD candidate to an unhappy housewife and mother of four.

While I stayed unhappy for many years, my story didn't end there.

I learned lessons. I made mistakes (some more than once), and I continued to believe that something else was waiting for me if I could only break free of the life I had been living on autopilot.

In the chapters that follow, I'll share the lessons that I learned to help me create a life that I love, as well as the tools I used to dismantle the stories that were keeping me stuck as an unhappy housewife.

The more women I share my story with, the more women nod their heads in agreement and say, "Yes! It feels just like that!" Many of us are fighting the same battles and share the same struggles, although we rarely like to talk about the gritty, vulnerable details.

I hope this book changes that.

I hope you find nuggets of your own story within mine.

I hope you know you're not alone and that this isn't all there is for your life.

I hope you decide to create a life that you love.

In the coming chapters, I will illustrate why growth and personal development are important in every phase of life and how to reimagine motherhood as a career rather than a never-ending to-do list.

I will encourage you to look closely at the communication within your marriage and break negative patterns that may keep you feeling stuck and unfulfilled. I will also remind you who YOU are and why you must learn how to prioritize your own health and self-care again, not only for your physical and mental well-being but because you and your family deserve the best version of you in this life.

It's true when they say, "There's nothing new under the sun." Many of the ideas and solutions I share with you in these pages aren't unique. Perhaps you are already perfectly aware of the fact that hiring someone to help with jobs around the house would take some of the tasks off your plate and create more time.

What is new, however, are the realizations I had throughout my journey and the hard questions I asked myself.

Why am I unwilling to hire a housekeeper even though my house is a disaster and I feel like I'm drowning in the laundry, toys, and dishes?

Why don't I want to have a date night with my husband?

Why does it feel like he can never hear me when I ask him for help?

Why do I feel so lost and unfulfilled when this is the life I asked for?

The answers to those questions and more didn't come easily. But when they came, and when I was truly willing to listen to them, they helped me finally catch my breath, find my voice, and regain my sanity.

These are lessons I learned the hard way.

I wasted many years of my life before I discovered these tools and, for that reason, I feel compelled to share them with you. I hope that you apply these lessons, entertain some new ways of thinking, and avoid that dangerous trap I fell into for so many years.

I hope you can learn from my mistakes, write your own story, and create a life you love today!

With Love,

Kirstin

www.kirstinsmith.com

INTRODUCTION

Hi. My name is Kirstin…and I'm a recovering unhappy housewife.

How did I become an unhappy housewife, you ask?

Well, it didn't happen overnight. I started out on this adventure as a spunky, optimistic young girl ready to change the world.

In 2012, I became a mom. While I had known for years that my husband and I would end up having a family, I wanted to create an impact in other ways, too.

When my first daughter was born, I was in my eleventh consecutive year of higher education and working on a PhD in Arabic and Islamic Studies.

It was, admittedly, an odd choice for a white girl from Kentucky.

My life, like many of us born in the 1970s and 1980s, was impacted by the events of 9/11/2001. The desire to understand those events and countless other foreign policy and international affairs issues followed me to college, where I quickly changed my major from Classical Ballet Performance to Religious Studies and Political Science.

I was always good at whatever field I focused on because I worked hard and applied myself. This personality trait has served me well throughout my life, my approach to motherhood, and my later attempts to turn my life around once I realized I had become an unhappy housewife.

When I was a student, I would travel to the Middle East or North Africa for three months every summer to be immersed in Arabic and improve my language skills. With years of effort, I finally hit those elusive targets of language proficiency – I could discuss abstract philosophical concepts and even dream in another language.

When the time came to apply to PhD programs, I was contacted by various programs that wanted to set up interviews. They sought me out and courted me. It felt like how high school football players get flown to campuses, taken on tours, and wined and dined…apparently, graduate programs do that for nerds, too. Who knew?

But when the time came to pivot to the land of diapers and burp cloths, I went all-in and withdrew from my PhD program to focus solely on my roles as a wife and new mom.

To be honest, I had grown frustrated with the climate on college campuses for years, and I didn't see it improving any time soon. My research dealt with justifications for violence in Islam, and I was heavily involved in conversations related to terrorism and suicide bombing. This was around the time when "Islamophobia" became a hot buzzword, often used to stifle viewpoints that diverged from the orthodoxy.

Ultimately, I got frustrated by those in academia who functioned as gate-keepers, determining who could have a voice on an issue based on their ethnicity or religious affiliation rather than their ability to read and interpret primary sources or put forth compelling, fact-based arguments and research.

I had also naively assumed that the Ivory Tower would be a place where truth could be pursued for truth's sake. I wasn't prepared for the post-9/11 political hot potato that was a specialization in Islamic Studies! Over time, I became increasingly exasperated and found myself dreading the days I had to set foot on campus.

Pulling the plug was an incredibly difficult decision for me, and I agonized about it for months…maybe even years.

I was scared.

Would I disappoint my colleagues? My advisor? My family and friends?

Who was I if I wasn't the nerdy girl who was perpetually in school and always traveling to the Middle East to study?

Eventually, I knew what had to be done, and I made the decision to withdraw.

Making the decision was the hard part. The transition itself wasn't a particularly difficult one because I had always envisioned myself in a role as a full-time or nearly full-time parent.

I was incredibly fortunate to grow up in a house with two loving parents, one of whom was a stay-at-home mom. My mom was there every afternoon when I got off the school bus. When I was young, she would wait for me at the bus stop, and we would walk home together. As I got older and gained a little more independence, she was still always home waiting for me with an after-school snack.

There were days we would sit right down in the middle of our 1980's linoleum kitchen and have a snack, leaning against the dark wood cabinets with their floppy brass pulls. In true kid fashion, unable to sit still, I would lay on the floor eating my snack and put my feet up on the cabinets.

This was our time to catch up: She asked me about my day, and I shared all the latest elementary school drama.

Growing up, this was a big deal to me, and I knew that I wanted to be there for my kids to come home to after school. Hell, that was a big part of why I had chosen a potential career in academia in the first place. I wanted to work "school hours" without working in K-12, so teaching at the college level seemed like a decent compromise that would allow me to work and also clock into my job as Mom by the late afternoon.

At the time, being home with one kid—especially when she was an infant who spent a good deal of time asleep—felt totally manageable. The majority of child- and home-related tasks fell on me because my husband, a natural entrepreneurial type, had his own baby in 2011: A gym that he opened and was spending long hours working in for the first few years.

While I played a support role from home in those early years, I never really considered myself to be "working." (Little did I know at the time how detrimental this way of thinking would prove to be.)

I took on all the overachiever Mom stuff: Pinterest boards full of playroom décor ideas, making baby food from scratch, cloth diapering, etc.

I had friends who were working moms. It seemed like a chaotic and stressful life to get young kids ready early in the morning, drop everyone off at daycare, go to work for a full day, pick the kids up, make dinner, and try to squeeze in some quality family time. They always seemed on edge and stressed. No way—I wanted no part of that.

To be perfectly honest, I thought my way was better.

And then the guilt started.

I felt guilty that I wasn't contributing to our household income.

I felt guilty that I wasn't contributing more to the world outside the four walls of my house.

I felt guilty that I had wasted people's time working on a PhD only to quit.

I felt guilty that I had let people down or disappointed them by not "living up to my potential."

I felt guilty for wanting a break from kids and kid-related stuff.

I felt guilty for taking time for myself when I got it.

I just felt guilty. All the time. For all the reasons.

Everyone has heard of mom guilt, and let me assure you, it's a very real thing.

As time went on, we kept adding more kids to the mix: A second…then a third…then a fourth.

I continued to sit in this place where I was constantly surrounded by my own guilt. I felt unfulfilled and conflicted: Why did I want to be away from these kids so badly, but the second I got away from them, they were all I could think about? *I wonder what they're doing right now… I should probably get back home and check on them…*

When you do something all day, every day, it is easy for it to consume your life or become your identity.

I was immersed in a world of playdates, Peppa Pig, and endless snacks. My husband, on the other hand, was immersed in an entirely different world: Building a business, managing employees for the first time, and keeping customers happy.

Our worlds and our roles became very defined…and very separate.

Things started to change, slowly at first, almost imperceptibly.

I grew resentful and frustrated.

I needed a break. I needed help. I felt lonely and underwater.

It felt like we were having the same argument over and over and over.

I felt as if I was always coming to him, nearly begging him to see me and recognize what was going on: "Please see how empty and exhausted I am from taking care of everyone else! Throw me some crumbs, anything. Just please love me and help me. Someone, please give back to me, so I don't feel so empty. This is unsustainable—I just can't keep this up. I don't know what to do!"

Granted, I didn't say it like that.

I felt the desperation inside. But when I tried to express it, it always ended up turning into that same old argument, which probably stemmed from something like him leaving his dirty clothes scattered all over the floor rather than in the laundry hamper.

What I wanted and needed him to hear was that I was lonely, lost, feeling unappreciated, and overlooked, but what he heard was, "Stop leaving your nasty, sweaty socks balled up, or you can wash your own goddamn laundry!"

Eventually, when the attempts to talk to one another and communicate what we needed kept turning into the same argument, it was easier to just not talk.

Kids in bed.

Show on Netflix.

Work/scroll on your computer or phone.

Get in bed.

Keep the peace.

Wash, rinse, and repeat.

There were times I would try to figure out how many days had gone by since we'd actually *spoken* to each other, anything more meaningful than a "What's for dinner?"

And then it happened.

I realized I was an unhappy housewife.

But maybe it was okay — after all, there seemed to be unhappy housewives all around me. Maybe we could help each other solve our problems and improve our lives! (There was that spunky, optimistic young girl again!)

With my older two kids in preschool and kindergarten at this point, I started putting more effort into building friendships with other mom friends I had met. As I got to know them, it turned out they were also unhappy housewives!

As I found more mom friends and joined some mom groups on social media to try and fight my way out of the wet paper sack of a life I was in, I started to notice some trends:

The vast majority of moms I knew seemed unhappy or, at least, somewhat unfulfilled.

They didn't speak very highly of their husbands. In fact, most of the time, their husbands were treated as just another kid to raise and clean up after.

They didn't particularly enjoy having sex with their husbands, either. They felt an obligation to do it to keep the peace and keep their husbands from getting overly pouty, but it was not gratifying or something they pursued because it lacked intimacy and connection. At best, it was just another item on their to-do list.

At the same time, they wanted to feel desired by their husbands.

They wanted to be treated well, appreciated, and even "wined and dined" occasionally on date night (but only if they didn't have to do all the planning for it).

They were tired.

They didn't have many interests outside of their kids.

The majority weren't in great physical shape and put little focus on their own health and well-being.

I realized I had become an unhappy housewife, surrounded by countless other unhappy housewives, and the future wasn't looking bright for any of us.

We were going through the motions of life: We cared for everyone; we made the necessary plans; we worked those to-do lists. But I couldn't help but feel disappointed by how things had turned out. And it appeared I wasn't alone in that sentiment.

Was this all there was?

All-day, every day? Just this same shit?

An eternal Groundhog Day of school pickup, doing the dishes, and being pissed off at our husbands?

Surely this wasn't why we were here on Earth? To just muddle along and go through the motions while being miserable and disconnected?

And then one day I asked myself:

What would this look like if I were happy?

CHAPTER ONE

THE UNPAID HOUSEKEEPER

Let's be honest: While different households might run in different ways, the fact of the matter is that women tend to the affairs of the home to a greater degree than men. In many houses, we shoulder the majority of work related to the cleaning, laundry, groceries, cooking, dishes, errand-running, child-wrangling, bathing, bedtime, etc.

Add a career or other obligations to that list, and you've got what seems like an unending list of to-do's calling your name.

But there's a unique element to these tasks for stay-at-home moms, too.

When my first child was born, my husband and I agreed that daycare wasn't an option we wanted to pursue. We lived in Texas, and our closest relatives were 1,000 miles away, so help from family members wasn't exactly an option either.

In hindsight, there wasn't a great deal of back-and-forth on the issue, as I knew I wanted to play a very active role in raising our kids every day.

In 2013, I made the decision to leave the career that I had spent a decade preparing for, and I fully committed to that homemaker life.

We've all heard the "soap operas and bon-bons" stereotype of stay-at-home moms. Having been one, I can assure you that perception couldn't be farther from the truth. There are elements of the job that are easier when a baby is younger; they sleep a majority of the day, and you have the ability to get to some things on your to-do list: Do a load of laundry, prepare a nice meal, or even take a leisurely stroll or get some exercise.

Eventually, those naps drop, and that baby becomes mobile.

What was once a sweet little bundle o' joy now becomes the neediest little terrorist who will ransack your Tupperware drawer 372 times per day. And when they're not destroying something, they are obsessed with anything that could potentially kill them.

I always felt a deep sense of gratitude toward my husband for his drive and determination to provide for us. We were beyond fortunate that I was able to choose to stay home and raise our children from the jump, but it didn't take long for me to feel the slightest, almost imperceptible wave of jealousy when he left the house for work.

It felt odd that this arrangement was something I had actively sought but, at the same time, I felt like a bit of a prisoner in my own home. I missed the predictability of a routine when I found myself waking at all hours of the night as my schedule was dictated by naps, diaper changes, and feeding times.

I missed being able to have a real conversation with an adult, someone other than our pediatrician, of course.

Some people have a tendency to attack a challenge head-on with 100% commitment. I decided if I wasn't going to work outside the house and produce the way I had anticipated, I was going to mom so hard that everyone would have no choice but to see my effort and shower me with praise and accolades.

It wasn't exactly that I *needed* external affirmation, but I was certainly used to it.

Transitioning from any field "out there" in the workforce to being a full-time mom results in an unsettling lack of certainty. There are no quarterly reviews. There are no grades. There are no promotions, increased sales revenues, or greater profit margins by which to measure your success.

In a sense, you're flying blind, making things up as you go along, and hoping you don't raise a serial killer.

I attacked my new career with the same hunger and drive with which I had attacked my previous career: I read all the books, I created ways to challenge myself, and I stepped into the grind consistently, day after day.

What did this look like, you ask? I'll tell you.

I decided if I was going to be Mom as a full-time job, I was going to mom harder than anyone had ever mommed before. I cloth diapered that baby. We practiced rolling over like she had Olympic aspirations. I made 97% of the food she consumed in that first year. I turned my kitchen into a science lab disaster of sauteed organic chicken liver and root vegetable purees.

I was doing the damn thing.

And you know what? It worked…for a bit.

My motivation and stubbornness carried me through for a little while, and I felt somewhat fulfilled. Don't get me wrong, I love my kids and enjoy spending time with them, but eventually, I started to feel like an unpaid chef, housekeeper, and nanny for my family.

By the time we had become a family of five, I was drowning in our home. The laundry, the messes, the food, all of it.

As the years went on, every meal that my kids turned up their noses at made me angry.

Did these people not realize how hard I worked for them?! Was a little appreciation too much to ask? Could I get a thank-you every once in a while?

When you shoulder the burden of the menial household tasks, you never get a thank you. Everyone loves having clean underwear in their drawer, but do they thank you for putting it there? Nope. Do they bitch when it's not there? Yep.

My husband would encourage me to think about getting a cleaning lady to help around the house, and I consistently pushed back. I'd give him various reasons, typically related to being private and not liking people in my space, sometimes citing the anticipated cost of hiring someone to help. But the real reason was that my identity had been wrapped up in my role as a stay-at-home mom for years. Deep down, I felt that hiring a cleaning lady was an acknowledgment that I couldn't do it all, and I wasn't ready to admit that.

Remember how I mentioned my stubbornness earlier? Yep, that led me to create one of the most disastrous stories about my marriage and emotional well-being.

Over the course of several years, those annoying habits that everyone has became a particular thorn in my side. My husband, not the tidiest person you've ever met, was certainly capable of picking up and cleaning things. Hell, I saw him do it inside his business, where he held a high standard of cleanliness when it came to his employees.

So why would he walk through the living room and kick the random kid cups, scattered shoes, or other miscellaneous items strewn about instead of just picking them up? Worse yet, at times, he would pick the shit up out of frustration and toss it across the room to another random spot on the floor. Hardly helpful and honestly — Infuriating.

Anyone with a man in the house already knows they can be a bit absent-minded during bathroom trips, especially if they're scrolling on their phone at the same time. Every time I noticed pee that was off-target, I was beyond annoyed.

These conversations would start off reasonably:

"Hey babe, if you dribble some pee, will you please wipe it up?"

"Hey babe, when you take your socks off, will you please not leave them crumpled up in a ball so I have to reach my hand in to fix them?"

"Hey babe, if you're going to pick that up, could you put it where it actually belongs and not just throw it to a new place?"

"Hey babe…"

You get the idea.

As time went on, I lost my patience and started internalizing the conversation. *What in the actual fuck? Can he hear me when I ask him these things? Why is this so hard? I'm doing all this work, and I asked for one simple thing. Oh yeah, he can hear me all right. He's doing this on purpose. There is no other explanation for it.*

And then, just like that, I created my first big story: *My husband doesn't value me or my efforts for our family. He treats me like a housekeeper/nanny that he also gets to sleep with. We are not teammates or equals in this life because, if we were, he would listen to me or help me with the [insert task here].*

Maybe you have made this your story or something similar. Maybe it's still yours.

Everywhere I looked, I could find evidence to support my story. It continued to play on repeat in my head until I was convinced of its truth.

Not only did I begin to feel more and more unappreciated, but I started to wield my responsibilities as a weapon.

For several years, our conversations looked like this:

Me: "I have to take so-and-so to the doctor on Thursday, but it's during the baby's naptime. Will you be around in the afternoon so I could maybe leave the younger ones here with you? Then I could run a couple of errands without having to take ALL the kids."

Jeff (with an exasperated sigh): "I'll have to check my calendar; I know I have a 10:30 meeting and a bunch of shit I have to get done because the accountant wants stuff for taxes, so I have to email the bookkeepers. And I was hoping to go to the gym...."

Me (now super annoyed and sarcastic): "Forget it, I'll just take them all and deal with having a cranky baby. Then I guess I'll just take all four of them to the grocery store and come home and fix dinner for everyone...."

At this point, any overture on his part didn't make a difference. I was going to do it the hard way, struggle, and let him see me struggle. I was also going to stay pissed off.

Most of the time, it felt like there was a bit of a Cold War in our house, and we used our to-do lists as a shield to deflect from criticism or as a weapon against the other person.

When I asked for some help with the house or the kids to create some space for myself, I felt like I always got confronted with proof of my husband's busy-ness. I started to do the same thing when he needed something from me or when I felt like I had to justify my request for his help.

I didn't realize that, by doing this, I was focusing on busy-ness over productivity and using it to get validation.

I didn't have a paycheck to bring home.

I didn't have 5-star Google reviews for my business to point to.

I didn't have performance reviews, a raise, or a promotion to show.

I had an endless to-do list of menial household tasks that no one seemed to see or appreciate.

If I gave those tasks to someone else, how would I be able to prove my contribution?

I needed to be busy all the time like my husband was.
I needed ammo in the pissing match of who was doing more.

As long as I was crossing off items on that world's longest to-do list, I felt like I was contributing. I felt like I was producing things I could point to and feel a sense of accomplishment, even on those hopeless days when I worked so hard to get the house perfect for a mere five minutes only to have a Tasmanian devil of a toddler destroy it again, right about the time my husband walked in the door.

If he was busy, I had to be busier.

How could I win a fight if I couldn't point to all the things I had to get done for our family? I was NOT about to give up my go-to weapon.

I had tied my worth and contribution as a woman, wife, and mother to household chores that, in the grand scheme of things, weren't important at all!

This need to stay busy came about as a result of our poor communication and an embarrassing lack of confidence in my own identity and contribution both to my family and the world at large.

I was playing small in life by continuing to think in terms of "busy" rather than "effective."

I was refusing to solve my own problem out of a stubborn desire to win hypothetical future arguments.

**I wanted to be right and feel justified
more than I wanted to be happy.**

After years of resisting the idea of getting a cleaning lady, I finally caved and hired someone to help. At the time, I did not have a grand realization about the use and worth of my time. Realistically, I was pregnant with baby #4 and sick and tired of cleaning up after my family. Blame it on the pregnancy hormones, but I was 100% over everyone and their shit.

It was time to bring in some resources. And man, oh man, was it worth it!

I could not have anticipated the opportunities and new ways of thinking that were about to open up for me.

CHAPTER TWO

WHAT LANGUAGE ARE YOU SPEAKING?

For many years, it felt like my husband and I were stuck and unable to communicate with one another. We had some real "men are from Mars, women are from Venus" vibes going. It was almost as if we weren't even speaking the same language. As it turns out, we weren't.

We were having the same arguments over and over: I would express my needs, wants, and desires only to feel like I was met with lip service or, worse yet, crickets.

My asks weren't huge:

"Can you help me by doing X, Y, or Z around the house?"

"Can you create some space for me to get away by watching the kids?"

"Can you put your phone down at the dinner table and help me with the kids?"

After years of having the same conversations with little to no progress, it truly felt like we didn't have a shared language with which to effectively communicate with one another.

I felt like I was expressing my needs clearly, but he would look at me as though I was speaking with a thick, European accent and just smile and nod.

Many of you have probably read (or at least heard of) the book *The Five Love Languages* by Gary Chapman. The author describes how different people speak different "love languages" to communicate with and show their love for others. These love languages are: Words of Affirmation, Physical Touch, Quality Time, Receiving Gifts, and Acts of Service.

Often, if you're not paying attention, you may express love to someone in the language that is most natural for you and how you prefer to receive love. However, this might not be the same language that your partner speaks, making it challenging for them to feel that love.

I HIGHLY recommend that you read the book or, at the very least, take the free quiz online to determine what your love language is. If you are married or in a relationship, take the time to discover your partner's love language as well. If I had done that, I would have realized what was going wrong in my marriage.

For years, the resentment and lack of connection that grew between my husband and me was a result of not being intentional about the languages we were using to express love to one another.

The little messes he made, the unwillingness to help me out more around the house, and the expectation that everything was just magically done throughout the day led me to a very resentful place where I ended up feeling like that unpaid nanny, housekeeper, and chef.

I served my family on a high level, always trying to anticipate their needs and fulfill them to show them they were loved. I prided myself on how hard I worked to care for them. However, I never felt like my work was appreciated or even acknowledged.

I had the house and kids at least marginally buttoned up most of the time, but my husband didn't seem to care about the time I spent or the effort I put in. So I worked harder and took on more tasks, subconsciously hoping he would see how hard I was working and register that it came from a place of deep love and commitment.

The more tasks I took on, and the more my feelings of being unappreciated grew, the more exhausted and frustrated I became. What I was doing was unsustainable; I had no time for myself, I was always busy, and there was always more work to be done.

I craved help. But, as you already know, I didn't want to hire a housekeeper.

I wanted my husband to be the one to help.
And I didn't just want him to help me.
I wanted him to *want* to help me.

It didn't feel meaningful to me if I had to ask for his help or instruct him on what needed to be done. I wanted him to see the task, anticipate my needs and desires, then act on them out of love for me and a desire to pitch in. But that rarely happened.

So I started telling myself a new story, day in and day out: *My husband doesn't want to help me. He doesn't care that I'm drowning. He can't be bothered to throw me a life preserver.*

If I had to ask or guilt him into helping, I didn't feel better. When I explained that I was feeling overwhelmed by all my duties and he suggested solving the problem with money, I was furious! I didn't want a housekeeper to help me; I wanted him to help me!

The problem was that, at the time, I couldn't understand why it was so important to me that my husband complete those tasks and help me out around the house. It wasn't simply that they needed to get done, or I would have hired a housekeeper. They meant more to me. Somehow, along this journey, the vacuuming, dishwashing, and laundry folding had picked up a meaning I didn't yet understand.

On the occasions when he did take some initiative and put a few dishes in the dishwasher or pick up the kid toys scattered around the kitchen and living room, I wasn't quick to give credit.

Instead, I wrote off his efforts as a tasteless attempt to score points that he would later attempt to cash in for sex like they were tokens from some risqué Chuck E. Cheese.

Damned if you do, damned if you don't, amirite?

The reason for this disconnect was rooted in love languages.

My primary love language is Acts of Service.

The most natural way for me to love the people around me is to serve them. I did this by pouring myself into our household every day: making sure the kids had warm, nutritious meals cooked for them, their favorite unicorn shirt was clean for school, crisp sheets were on their beds, etc.

But here's the problem – my husband and kids didn't speak that love language.

While I was beating myself up, martyring myself, and bending over backward to serve them, all my effort to make them feel loved was wasted because I was only loving them the way I wanted to be loved and the way that came most naturally to me.

Each of them has a love language unique to them, and my efforts were falling on deaf ears.

I wanted my husband to pitch in and do the dishes for me because I speak Acts of Service. This is my primary love language and the way that I, most naturally, express my love for those I care about. It really wasn't enough that he *did* the work to help me; I needed him to *want* to do the work to help me. He had to *want* to because it meant it was out of love, not a sense of obligation, or in an attempt to keep score.

By contributing his time and energy, he would make me feel cared for, loved, and valued, just as I had tried to make him feel by contributing my time and energy. But it's just not the same when you tell someone to wash the dishes so you will feel loved, and they wash the dishes. I wanted him to see that the dishes needed to be done, actively think about how he could show me his love by helping to do them, and then help me of his own accord.

However, my husband (like many husbands!) speaks fluent Physical Touch, not Acts of Service.

He spent years trying to love me in his own way, the way he wanted to receive love, and I wasn't very good at receiving it or giving it in that language.

Just like I didn't want him to do the dishes out of a sense of duty, he didn't want me to treat sex like it was just another thing to cross off my to-do list, which, to be honest, I was guilty of a lot of the time. He wanted me to *want* to do it. *Initiate* it. Use physical touch to make him feel cared for, loved, and valued.

Even after we both read the book and identified our love languages, it still took some time to realize how this dynamic was playing out within our house and how unintentionally selfish we were being.

I was so consumed by expressing and receiving love via Acts of Service that I was resentful when my efforts weren't appreciated. And I was disappointed when my husband wasn't completely blown away by my all-encompassing love with every pair of freshly-matched socks he pulled out of his drawer.

I was exhausted and begging for help. I wanted someone to love me and give me a break by pitching in and making me feel like I was on a team and not the solo player who kept everything running pseudo-smoothly.

However, my husband was loving me in his own way, but I was unable to see it. He was speaking to me in Physical Touch when he would smack my ass in the kitchen, kiss me goodbye, or seek intimacy and connection through sex.

He wanted to be loved by me the same way, and I was dropping the ball. I'm not huge on physical touch, to begin with, and as a mom of young kids who always wanted to be all over me, I was touched-out most days. The ass-grabs were annoying, I didn't feel connected outside or inside the bedroom, and my husband's second love language (Words of Affirmation) rang hollow as I was too wrapped up in my own pity party to hear that he was telling me I was loved and appreciated.

It's one thing to identify your love language, but it's another thing entirely to put it into practice and make a conscious effort to love your partner in THEIR language.

Initially, my husband and I read the book, took the quiz, identified our individual languages, and then moved on with our days. There was no practical application to use this tool to improve our relationship.

Eventually, my husband realized that I don't speak Physical Touch and, while he still smacks my ass 4,528 times a day, he made a much more concerted effort to serve me and our family with his time and effort.

As a matter of fact, I start every day with gratitude, and one of the first things on my list is that my husband makes a cup of coffee and brings it to me.

Acts of service, baby! Now we're talking!

Likewise, I eventually stopped tying my household work to the feeling of being unappreciated because I realized it wasn't his love language. If I stopped cooking, cleaning, or folding laundry, my husband wasn't going to feel less loved or cared for. And he definitely wasn't going to stop loving me.

And while it doesn't come naturally for me, sometimes I have to get inside my own head and yell, "Kirstin!! Just shut up and touch him!!" The best use of my time is making my husband feel loved and appreciated by initiating physical touch (of all varieties) and using affirmative words that express my gratitude and appreciation for him. The more loved he feels, the better he can love me.

This was not an easy lesson for us, but it was one that improved our relationship and communication in a drastic way. Once we became intentional about which languages we were speaking and what we were expecting the other person to speak back to us, we were finally able to hear what the other person had been saying.

CHAPTER THREE

THE NEGATIVE CYCLE POLKA

Why do we keep having the same fight over and over?

I lost count of how many times I asked myself that question.

It always seemed that the conversation started in a good place. I had a sincere intention to express my needs and communicate how I was feeling with my partner so that we could both grow and be happy.

Despite my great intentions, it always seemed to escalate. I could not understand why my simple requests for help, support, attention, and time were met with resistance. Why couldn't he just listen to me, HEAR me, and then do what I was asking him to do?

Instead, this is what a typical conversation looked like in our house:

Me: Would you mind not leaving your dirty clothes on the floor and just tossing them in the hamper?

Jeff: Sure, where's the hamper?

Me: (Now *extremely* triggered): Are you kidding? It's this thing right here…it's literally been sitting in the same spot for the last three years.

Jeff: Okay.

Silence.

Me: (Even more triggered): I spend all day cleaning up other people's messes. The last thing I need is to follow you around and clean up your messes, too. I mean, I'm the one doing all the laundry...

Jeff: I have a lot going on, too, you know!

Me: No one said you didn't!

Agitate, agitate, agitate until we were both pissed off, feeling unappreciated, and frustrated.

That was the dance. And we went dancing on the regular, rehearsing it with increasing frequency as the years ticked by.

Every time we repeated the same old argument, I became convinced a new story was true: *My husband doesn't care about my needs. He doesn't value me; he doesn't love me, and he doesn't want to help me feel happy and fulfilled in life.*

The more I repeated this story in my mind, the more evidence I found to prove its validity. It became a self-fulfilling prophecy that undermined our relationship time and time again.

What neither one of us could recognize at the time was that we were caught in the middle of a vicious negative cycle, and it was our default pattern of communication.

We stayed trapped, constantly repeating the same cycle in our communication, unable to recognize the difference between primary and secondary emotions. Primary emotions are those that occur instantaneously and automatically following a particular event, whereas secondary emotions are those cascading emotions that gradually emerge as our brains try to make sense of that event.

Typically, when we argue or act out our emotions with our partner, we are dealing in secondary emotions: Anger, humiliation, resentment, anxiety, worry, helplessness, etc. However, these emotions on display are just the tip of a much larger emotional iceberg.

What we don't see is the huge mass of ice under the surface: Those deep primary emotions like fear, sadness, and shame.

When, for various reasons, we cannot express those primary emotions, we will act out the secondary emotions. When we feel sadness or fear, that might come across as anger directed at our partner. If we're experiencing feelings of shame and unworthiness, we may withdraw and distance ourselves.

All it takes is one small trigger to start the negative cycle dance each time: A tone of voice, a facial expression, a sarcastic comment. You know, that thing that happens and always makes you think to yourself, *oh great...here we go again.*

These cycles usually follow patterns based on how each person behaves. We happened to follow the most common type of negative cycle where I pursued connection (good or bad), and my husband would distance himself.

Before every jump back onto the roller coaster of our negative cycle, my stories would rattle around inside my head: *Relationships are supposed to be fifty-fifty. I'm definitely giving my 50 percent. Why can't he ever muster up his 50 percent? Why can't he reach across the table, or cross that proverbial line, to meet me and work with me? Why do I feel like I'm working so hard and he won't prioritize our relationship?*

The more that these emotions and stories swirled in my head and the more that we engaged in this pattern, the more my husband withdrew, becoming quieter and quieter. I got even less of what I was craving from him, which was connection, safety, and security.

Every repetitive argument consisted of me attempting to establish some connection with the person I loved and felt so far away from.

Let's be honest; anyone with kids knows that sometimes they act out to get attention. And sometimes, any attention can be better than no attention. Well, as much as we might like to think we outgrow that tendency, it's not necessarily true. Old habits die hard.

I was feeling all the feelings. But I was unable to express the TRUE feelings or PRIMARY feelings I was dealing with, and that led me to bring up the laundry, the help with the kids, or the general feeling of drowning.

I couldn't explain to him that I was immensely sad.

I was questioning my purpose, and I was disappointed about the things I had given up to become a stay-at-home mom. I wasn't fully aware of how I felt, so I tended to express the daily frustration that I was dealing with in the form of tedious chores and household labor. That was why I always felt so well-intended; I was truly attempting to find a solution to problems that I knew had to be dealt with, but my attempts to fix things only made things worse.

Our dance looked like this:

I would make a demand or an ask from my partner. Sometimes perfectly reasonable or innocuous, but he never liked my tone. *Trigger.* I never liked his facial expression. *Trigger.*

I feared the distance between us and always felt like I was working to create more closeness and bring us together as a team, so his non-response would trigger me further. It wasn't just that it annoyed me or made me angry; it legitimately felt threatening.

It was as if I was coming to him, making an attempt, holding my hand out to him, and being met with a casual shrug. He would distance himself…and I couldn't allow that. It was an existential threat when I couldn't get him to talk to me or understand what I was asking him for.

At this point, the inner child comes out: "Oh, you don't want to talk to me? OK. I'll *make* you talk to me." After all, some attention is better than no attention, right?

My steps in this back-and-forth dance touched on blame, criticism, anything necessary to get a response from him. There was a level of desperation: I cannot let him just drift away—I have to see some emotion to prove that it's still there! I craved some sort of emotional connection so badly that I didn't care if it was good or bad. I needed to know that we were going to be okay, that our relationship was salvageable.

In hindsight, we followed a fairly predictable pattern: night after night of disconnecting after the kids were in bed, TV on, scrolling on phones instead of talking to one another. After so many nights of that, an inevitable blow-up brewed. I didn't know how else to break through the distance and see if he was still there with me, so I'd bring up what I needed, often insinuating he wasn't supporting me.

We knew the dance, so we danced it. Then we went back to nights on end without really speaking.

In many relationships, this pattern plays out the same way. Typically, men will withdraw from perceived conflict, so they play the role of Distancer.

Women, on the other hand, tend to be less hesitant to engage emotionally than men are, so we often play the role of Pursuer.

The Pursuer genuinely means well. She is reaching for her partner and trying to bridge the perceived distance that she feels in the relationship. However, by continuing to dance within the negative cycle, the Pursuer is reinforcing and even exacerbating the distance in the relationship. As you can probably guess, that increasing distance only served to reinforce my beliefs and stories about my husband, as well as increase the fear I felt around that distance.

Typically, the Pursuer's primary emotions stem from feeling alone, sad, and fearful. This is why I sought security through connection. The fear of being left alone, rejected, or abandoned is distressing and causes this cycle to repeat itself ad nauseam.

If I give up, I'm afraid you'll leave, and I'll feel even more alone.

If I can get close to you and feel like I matter, I'll be okay.

The problem is not the Pursuer or the Distancer. The problem is the dance. The negative cycle itself.

As long as we continued to speak about and exhibit our secondary emotions, we were stuck doing the same stupid dance.

Being able to reach new levels of vulnerability with one another allowed us to tap into a deeper level and get into the nitty-gritty, all the stuff we had glossed over for so many years.

Simple, but not easy.

To be fair, this was a lesson we would never have learned had we not committed to marriage counseling. We were both prideful, stuck in our ways, and slow to acknowledge that our relationship needed work. But eventually, we overcame our perceived social stigmas and committed to bringing in an unbiased third party to bridge that gap and help us understand why the other person could never simply listen to what we were saying without starting a fight.

Marriage counseling was a last-ditch effort to try and hear what the other person was saying.

I think we both knew, deep down, that what we were doing wasn't working. Neither one of us was happy nor fulfilled in our marriage. At the same time, neither one of us was going to be the one to throw in the towel, so to speak. Most of the time, we were stuck in the muddy middle. Our marriage ranked about a 5 on a scale of 1 to 10: Bad enough to know it could be better, but good enough to suck it up and keep trudging along with the status quo.

It took all of two seconds for our counselor to point out our negative cycle. Once he described it back to us, we each had a lightbulb moment. We were stuck on the surface and only communicated in secondary emotions. It was why we stayed pissed off, resentful, and angry.

It took time and effort to get used to expressing our primary emotions with one another. After all, we hadn't done a great deal to engender trust over recent years, and meaningful, honest conversations require vulnerability.

While we worked on expressing our primary emotions, we also worked on anticipating and understanding each other's primary emotions even when they weren't being vocalized.

When I could look past my husband's tendency to lash out at me and come off as angry, I could see the fear or shame that was often driving that behavior. Reminding myself what his primary emotions might be allowed me to be more sympathetic and take his actions less personally than I had before. It allowed me to let things roll off my back, whereas, in the past, I would've confronted them head-on with a defiant argument or taken them personally as a sign that I had done something wrong.

It didn't have to be all about me or our relationship anymore. It allowed me to recognize the struggles and fears he dealt with personally and vice versa.

Don't get me wrong, it's hard to teach an old dog new tricks.

We've worn our dancing shoes for so many years that when the music comes on, we still tend to fall back into old behaviors.

It takes constant effort and introspection to examine what is showing up as anger or resentment and determine what the underlying emotion at play truly is. However, when we recognize it, we can respond to that instead of the anger or resentment.

CHAPTER FOUR

WHO AM I?

To this day, I still remember coming home from school as an elementary-aged kid and finding my mom at home waiting for me. No matter what had happened that day, good or bad, she was there to get me a snack and listen attentively while I told her all about it.

When I was young, my mom found a way to contribute to our household income by working from home as an owner-operator in her own business. Being extremely detail-oriented and meticulous about cleaning and repairs, she specialized in restoring old Wurlitzer jukeboxes and selling them for a decent profit. I was always impressed by how she managed to be home with me but still work on these projects and contribute in her own way.

Mom had a knack for sales, so years later, when I entered adolescence, she went to work in real estate and created success as a producer in her own right. We would always describe her with that line from *Tommy Boy*, saying she could sell a ketchup popsicle to a woman in white gloves.

But even as she established her own career, she still found ways to keep me involved and stay active and present in my life.

These fond memories followed me into adulthood. I knew clearly that I wanted to spend that after-school time with my kids.

This time was romanticized in my mind: Sitting in the middle of the kitchen floor just like in my childhood memories, sharing an after-school snack, belly laughing about all the stories we were sharing. Like it was straight out of a commercial for string cheese or some other snack food.

There was a period between my first child's birth and my decision to withdraw from my PhD program when I toyed with the idea of finishing my degree *and* pursuing that career I had invested so much time and energy in. Initially, I decided to juggle them both to see if I could do it all.

Luckily, I had completed all my coursework and qualifying exams at that point and was deep in the middle of a translation project that was intended to serve as the basis for my dissertation. Most of my work was independent and could be completed at home.

However, I was still teaching.

I had agreed several years earlier to help former US Ambassador Edward Djerejian, who was serving as the director of the Baker Institute for Public Policy, develop and teach his first upper-level course on Middle Eastern Policy. While I no longer attended and actively co-taught the classes, I was still meeting with him occasionally for grading, planning, and status updates.

Picture me, a brand-new mom, readying myself for one of our scheduled meetings. I strap my perpetually sleepy newborn onto my torso with a baby carrier and hit that meeting, no problem.

I've got this! I can do it all! I can have it all!

This particular meeting was a bit out of the ordinary because we had a third attendee: Former Secretary of State James A. Baker.

We conducted our business, set up our action items, and were in the middle of telling a few stories and making small talk when my baby woke up from her nap. She proceeded to squirm a bit, and then, with a giant stretch, she let out one of those massive, incredibly noisy, and incredibly *explosive* newborn poops.

This was a bad one. All over her and all over me, all while two high-ranking US diplomats stared at me with eyes as big as saucers.

That day was a turning point for me, and I started to tell myself a new story.

My new story was: *I can't have it all; I can't possibly juggle raising kids and having a career. This is a binary; an either-or. Something has to go.* And the choice was made.

I made the decision to withdraw from my PhD program and leave my entire way of life in exchange for a new one. It was scary and uncertain, but I definitely looked forward to telling my first-born daughter about how she pooped her pants in front of a Secretary of State when she got older!

It was a huge decision and a meaningful transition in my life. I had spent a decade in higher education and traveled to remote corners of the Middle East to support my academic and career goals. It felt odd to take a large part of my identity away, but I couldn't fathom a way to keep one foot in both worlds, especially with this new story firmly rooted in my mind.

So there I was. At home. With a baby. Alone.

At the same time, my husband began his entrepreneurial journey and was working long, difficult, and often unpredictable hours to make ends meet and get a fledgling business off the ground. During the first couple of years, I vividly remember moving a high chair into the bathroom so I could bathe baby #1 in the evenings while I fed baby #2.

It wasn't an uncommon occurrence for me to run through dinner, clean-up, baths, and the full bedtime routine and have both kids in bed before my husband was even home from work.

There didn't seem to be any break or any breathing room. I was on the proverbial hamster wheel, and the pressure was building. There was no family nearby to lean on, and babysitters were often unreliable, not to mention expensive for a one-income household that had just started a business.

Things I used to take for granted now seemed like utter impossibilities.

I'd love to get a haircut. But who will watch the kids?

I'd love to go work out...after all, my body doesn't exactly look like it used to. But who will watch the kids?

I felt myself starting to get a little burned out, and I *craved* some kid-free time. However, something strange happened when I got that kid-free time: I had a hard time disconnecting from my kids, even when they weren't right next to me.

I didn't get a ton of kid-free time; let's be real here. Usually, it was something dull, like a solo trip to the grocery store. Not exactly an extravagant getaway, but I would seize the opportunity! However, when I was gone, I found myself worrying about them or feeling oddly guilty about leaving them with my husband, even if it was only for a short time.

Eventually, when the kids got a bit older, I enrolled them in a Mother's Day Out program to give me a few kid-free time blocks during my week. At this point, I felt like I had been serving a form of solitary confinement for years, locked inside my home with these little people. Now, here I was on the outside with the ability to make some "mom friends."

You know how it goes: We would see each other at preschool drop-off day after day and maybe discover we had something in common (other than having made a kid or two) and potentially hit it off.

Next thing you know, you're grabbing coffee after drop-off or some cocktails at a happy hour and commiserating about the current challenges with your kids or struggles, trying to get everyone in the family on the same page.

At the time, it seemed perfectly natural that those conversations always gravitated toward our families and the struggles we had as moms. I mean, we were in the shit!

But as I look back on them, there were rarely any conversations about us as women or unique individuals: our goals, our desires, what made us feel good and happy.

It was almost as if we had lost the ability to talk about those things. Being consumed by our (relatively) new roles in life as moms was challenging. We were attempting to figure it all out, support our husbands, raise happy and healthy children, and keep our houses in order. But we were forgetting to take time to care for ourselves.

We stopped prioritizing ourselves and taking care of ourselves as the assets we truly were, but we were the proverbial glue holding this shitshow together.

The same thing happened when my husband and I had time together, just the two of us. We talked to each other about the kids, not each other. Don't get me wrong, parents need to communicate about their children and their needs, concerns, and development. But those conversations cannot happen at the expense of checking in with and communicating with one another, just like you did before kids.

Everyone knows a couple whose kids have graduated high school and left the nest. As an outsider, you might be shocked to hear they're getting divorced after 20-something years of marriage. Every time I saw this, I was always perplexed: *You've had 20 years of practice to get this thing figured out — what took so long to make this decision? Were you simply waiting for the kids to leave this whole time?*

In those situations, there was often a husband working and consumed with his career in addition to a wife at home dealing with most of the child-rearing responsibilities.

Over an extended duration of time, when we consistently take a portion of ourselves and invest it outside ourselves, we begin to lose our identity. Dad's identity starts to become work, while Mom's identity starts to become the kids. If they fall into the trap of treating their marriage like a houseplant on a shelf, with little to no nurturing, it's not surprising how things play out once those kids leave.

Part of this stems from a natural tendency. When we take on a new task or role, especially one as important as becoming a mother, we may become a little obsessed with doing it well. Usually, this obsession with the details wanes over time—case in point, the difference between brand-new parents and the seasoned parents of two, three, four, or more kids.

However, another element may fuel the tendency for a husband to immerse himself in work and a wife to immerse herself in the kids.

**We naturally direct our energy to the area
where we know how to get a win.**

It was difficult for me to get a win on date night with my husband. I attempted to make a connection and check in with whatever was going on in his life. From my perspective, the low-hanging fruit was to ask about work: "How are things going at the gym?" "How are things going with clients?" "Employees?"

This ended up being like one of those old *Choose Your Own Adventure* books from growing up:

"If you caught Jeff on a bad day, turn to page four."

This would result in an almost immediate blow-up or negative cycle trigger: *Here I am just trying to make conversation, but he's giving me that same look again; what a dick....*

"If you caught Jeff on a good day, turn to page 12."

The conversation might last a little while. Perhaps he'd open up about a problem he was dealing with. Then I'd weigh in because, you know, I thought we were having a conversation.

This was rarely good. Between his personal listening and the stories about his own shame or embarrassment, we almost always ended up at the same place where yet another negative cycle would be triggered.

Our conversations and attempts to connect just weren't working. I felt like I was constantly tiptoeing around him because he was moody and unpredictable. I didn't have the emotional maturity at the time or the self-confidence to realize or appreciate the pressure he was under. Instead of calmly expressing my displeasure at his word choice or his unreasonable reaction to something I had said, I clammed up and internalized his shortness or crabbiness as indicative of something I had done wrong. In reality, most of the time, it didn't have anything to do with me.

Over time, I subconsciously chose to put more and more of my energy into my kids because I knew what to do and how to get a win with them.

The constant tension within our relationship led my husband to choose to put more and more of his energy into work because he knew what to do and how to get a win there. This only served to fuel my resentment and jealousy toward the business we owned; in many ways, it felt like the "other woman" in the relationship who got the best of my husband's energy, time, and focus.

It was easier to pull those levers in our own respective spheres than achieve success in our relationship and work toward improving the areas where we fell short.

**After some time, a new story emerged.
Only this time, it wasn't *just* a story. It was an identity.**

I am a mom.

The biggest side effect of this gradual shift in focus was my personal disconnect with who I was outside of being a mom. I lacked that connection with my husband, which also served to connect me to my pre-kid life.

So, I ask you: what makes you *you*?

Is it that you're a mom?

No offense, but that's really not that impressive or unique. Look around you; most women are moms. If they're not right now, there's a pretty good likelihood they will be in the future.

I don't mean to come off as insensitive to anyone who has struggled with pregnancy and infertility. Prior to having four kids, I was once on the receiving end of an infertility diagnosis; I have experienced the pain of miscarriage and the multi-year struggle of getting pregnant. I understand the road is not always an easy one.

But ladies: We can still be great moms and love our kids without making them our entire identity.

In fact, I would argue that our whole family would be a lot better off if we resisted that tendency to lose our identity to our children.

I guarantee, if someone were to ask you, "Who is [insert your first name here]?" most of you would come up with an answer that had something to do with you being a mom.

You are more than a mom.

You are more than a wife.

Sure, this life is challenging and demanding, and it might feel like it's consuming you, but there is still a girl inside you who might love to dance, play music, make art, or travel. She might be very quiet right now because no one has checked in on her in a very long time – neither you nor your spouse.

You might miss that girl and realize that she's slowly fading away, but it is your responsibility, and not anyone else's to check on her and remind her that this is still her life to live.

Let's be honest, when we become a mom, there is a tremendous amount of learning and growing that has to happen. You're thrown into a job where you must take care of every single physical and emotional need for a complete stranger with MASSIVE consequences for getting things wrong, and there is ZERO on-the-job training or instruction manual to help you do it successfully.

The job is all-consuming and if you're not careful, you will start to drift.

You will forget who you are.

Not only is being a mother hard—being in a relationship is hard, too! If you're losing yourself, experiencing emotional overwhelm, and dealing with the trials and tribulations of a marriage, it is easy to become frustrated with or resentful toward your husband if he's not actively checking on you and encouraging you to take care of yourself.

If you've each retreated to your respective spheres because it feels like you can't get the wins with each other, this only serves to exacerbate the problem.

We tend to forget that Dad is often dealing with his own struggles and a sense of societal or financial pressure as he gets used to his new position and responsibilities in life, as well.

It is 100% our responsibility to make sure we aren't losing our sense of self. This cannot be a task that we pass off to someone else. Use your support system but take responsibility for keeping yourself present and enlisted in this new growth.

We must do a better job of setting aside all the hats we wear (mom, wife, cook, housekeeper, laundry lady) and remember to put on the one that makes you *you*!

CHAPTER FIVE

THE FIVE PHASES OF A MARRIAGE

Everything you think you know about marriage is wrong.

Cinderella meets her prince, and they live happily ever after, right?

Sleeping Beauty is awakened by her prince's kiss, and they ride off on horseback into the sunset.

Tale as old as time.

Is it any wonder so many marriages are doomed from the start? I mean, look at what we're given as models from an early age.

What happens when Prince Charming becomes consumed with work after leaving his princess home exhausted with small children all day, then casually rolls in bitching about how dinner isn't ready yet without taking his eyes off his iPhone? Or when he gets a little too friendly with a co-worker on a work trip after Happy Hour? Mark my words, it's not always happily ever after.

How does the fairy tale couple handle it when they reach a point of emotional distance (or worse yet, an active dislike for one another) and they live more as roommates than lovers or partners?

I don't have to tell you the stats on divorce in the United States; everyone knows that divorce is commonplace. The vast majority of married couples either wind up divorced or have at least entertained the possibility at some point.

Unless you came from a family that clearly modeled what a successful and healthy marriage looks like, what blueprint does society give us to ensure that our marriages will be successful?

This is highly problematic because, at some point, you and your significant other will likely hate each other. Like the "Why-do-you-have-to-breathe-like-that?!" or "When-you-touch-me-I-want-to-punch-you-in-the-face" kind of hate.

Yep, a divorce is usually necessary. But maybe not in the way you've been taught.

Garrett J. White, entrepreneur, and founder of the Wake Up Warrior movement, hosts a podcast with his wife, Danielle (founder of DKW Styling in Laguna Beach), aptly titled *Date Your Wife*. Sometimes irreverent and brutally honest, it's part instructional, part motivational, and part therapy.

As the *Date Your Wife* podcast grew over time, Garrett J. White expanded on a new idea: All marriages will require a divorce. The reason for this is due to the natural evolution of a marriage into five stages:

1. Seduction – Everyone knows this phase, and everyone loves this phase. This is the "butterflies in your stomach, spontaneous sex, I only have eyes for you" phase. Your significant other can do no wrong and has no flaws. You get that schoolgirl giddiness and break into a grin when he calls or texts you.

2. Suffocation – Now you've been together a while. It turns out that not everything your partner does is the cutest, after all. You know that way he constantly leaves his shoes and socks in the middle of the room or slurps soup out of a spoon? Yeah, not wild about that, but it's okay. You still have enough of the seduction phase lingering to distract you from those relatively minor annoyances.

3. Strangulation – You've been together for a longer while and are now FIRMLY out of the seduction phase. There is no courting, no dating, no one making you feel special. You may exist as roommates at this point. Maybe you have sex semi-regularly out of a sense of obligation or just to keep the other person from getting too grouchy, but there's not really any connection there. The distance between you feels vast and insurmountable. Surely there's more to a relationship than this, right? You might even start to think, maybe I'm just with the wrong person.

This distance is what ends most relationships. Women tend to turn to the kids and focus their energy on the children's needs once the marriage feels like a lost cause. Men tend to focus on work, often numbing their unfulfilled needs with alcohol, porn, or even other women. This gap presents a danger zone for every married couple and is generally the point at which they call it quits and opt for a divorce. I mean, obviously, you're just not in love with each other anymore, right?

Remember our shitty cultural models for a happy marriage? They don't tell us how to bridge this gap and continue to evolve. They don't even tell us that this gap exists and is perfectly normal!

But my friends, it exists. And if you're not there yet, it will come.

We stayed in the strangulation phase for years. We longed for the golden days of seduction—hell, we would've gladly gone back to suffocation. But we didn't know how to get back there. Nothing we tried hit home. We didn't have a clear idea of how to move forward.

My story became: *A marriage shouldn't be this difficult. It shouldn't be this unenjoyable. At least, not if you're with the right person.*

While many people opt for a literal divorce at this point, the other option is a symbolic and figurative divorce whereby you break from your previous patterns, stories, and methods of interaction and CHOOSE to love each other again.

4. Submission – Maybe you've spent 10 years having the same fight over those socks and shoes in the middle of the floor, and the repetition has led you to believe deep down that your partner doesn't value you as a human being (I know I did). While you might be able to write a book on his flaws and shortcomings, you might also think of yourself as a blameless martyr. In this phase, you must take a step back and acknowledge that he's not the only one who has played a role in getting your relationship to this point. Odds are, you're not easy to be married to, either. Sure, he hasn't made you feel like a highly-valued, desirable woman, but have you made him feel like a highly-valued, desirable man? Sometimes it can be easy to get so wrapped up in our own needs and emotions that we forget how much we might be hurting our partners by not showing up for them.

We're quick to judge others by their actions, but we judge ourselves by our intentions.

---

5. Salvation – When you and your partner can acknowledge the things you have both done wrong, how you both have hurt one another, and how you each have done (or not done) things that contributed to the current state of your marriage, you can move

forward. As Garrett J. White explains, you divorce that young, immature marriage and bridge the gap together into a new marriage that is rooted in mutual respect and deeper trust. This is where the magic happens.

The idea of continuously choosing to be all-in on your relationship and marriage is too often glossed over in the fairy tales of the world.

My husband's "Aha!" moment came from the realization that he had worked tirelessly to convince me to marry him only to put our relationship up on a shelf like a houseplant. Our marriage didn't get watered frequently, but it was like a trusty old philodendron, and it was hard to kill.

It didn't get much water or sunlight. No one talked to it and told it how beautiful its leaves were. Before long, the once-strong houseplant was withering and looking rather pathetic.

It never occurred to him that he needed to work at our marriage, continue to choose our marriage, and nurture our marriage. Since he had not come from a background that provided the example of a strong marriage, he assumed it was a set-it-and-forget-it kind of thing. As the years ticked by, he shifted his focus to the other things he was working on: Raising kids and working on growing as a leader and business owner. From my perspective, it started to feel like he couldn't care less if I was around or not.

Personally, while I was more aware of the need to work on our relationship, I was just as guilty of allowing our relationship to stay gasping for air in the strangulation phase for way too long.

Relationships of any kind are hard. They require work. It gets monotonous, but like anything in life that you want to improve, you have to actively choose to put your time and energy into your relationship if you want the big payoff.

It's easy to be in love when it's a novelty. The test comes when that infatuation starts to fade—and, trust me, over time, it *will* fade. You must choose to bridge the gap and love in a new way. This requires concerted effort, intentional communication, and (perhaps most importantly) extreme vulnerability and honesty.

You might be thinking: *This is all fine and dandy, Kirstin. I get this whole "bridge the gap" thing, but how do I actually DO it?!*

Just like many things in life, the answer is simple. But that doesn't mean it's easy.

The first tool we utilized to bridge our gap and move out of the suffocation phase we were stuck in was to institute a regular date night.

Date night wasn't a thing in our house for the longest time. I knew it was probably a good idea, and I'm willing to bet my husband thought the same, but we had young kids and more excuses than motivation. We would talk about it, but we really never made it happen.

The kids are too little. We don't have any family nearby to watch them. I don't know any babysitters I trust. We don't have the money to pay a babysitter and go out to dinner!

Years went by where we didn't have much alone time—and when we *did* get some, our conversation ended up strained and awkward, with the kids as the default conversation topic.

No wonder neither one of us felt loved and appreciated; it felt like we couldn't be bothered to prioritize time for one another!

No wonder it felt like we weren't speaking the same language; we had allowed ourselves to fall out of practice because we hadn't carried on a real conversation in what seemed like years.

It's easy to fall into a pattern where you aren't willing to take on the additional responsibility of planning and executing a regular date night.

However, ladies: if we love and value our kids, we MUST take responsibility for the health and strength of our relationships with our husbands.

It's easy to think that we would do anything for our kids and for their well-being, but if you're not dating your husband and continuing to nurture that relationship through life's turbulent times, you are doing your children and your family a disservice.

I heard a quote once that opened my eyes to the truth in this concept: "If the marriage makes it, the family will make it, but the reverse isn't necessarily true."

The family you've built will NOT make it without feeding your marriage. It is the foundation you provide for your children and the model that will teach them how to love and be loved in the future.

Make date night a regular occurrence. Put it on both of your schedules so you can plan for it every week. Do not allow it to be something that gets filled in around other obligations; it is something that goes on your calendar first.

Don't have any family around? Get a babysitter for a couple of hours. Even if money is tight, the return on investment is huge.

Talk to one another. Be intentional. If you're in a rough spot in your relationship and this is a challenge, push through to the other side. I promise it will be worth it.

We've already touched on the second major tool we utilized: communication.

Are you communicating and acting out your secondary emotions? Does your partner see your frustration, anger, and/or resentment? What are you really feeling that you're not comfortable telling him?

Make the conscious effort to identify your primary emotions (fear, sadness, or shame) and communicate them honestly and from a place of vulnerability.

The same is true in reverse. My husband isn't the best at identifying his primary emotions and expressing them in the heat of the moment. He still has a default asshole mode that he can slip into pretty easily. However, I've stopped taking it personally.

I know when I see anger and frustration, something deeper is under the surface. Maybe he just got off the phone and received distressing news. Maybe he's stressed out about something in one of our businesses that I'm not aware of. The point is it is selfish to think it is always about me. Most of the time, it has absolutely zero to do with me. I just happen to be in front of him.

No one likes to be snapped at or be on the receiving end of a bad attitude and, in a perfect world, our partners would always be respectful and keep their emotions well-sorted and compartmentalized. However, we are not perfect creatures, and that is an unrealistic expectation.

There are times when I lose my patience with my husband, kids, dog, or random customer service representative due to something going on in my life that has absolutely ZERO to do with them.

Give each other some grace.

The health of your marriage will improve when you are able to stop taking things personally. Allow your partner to have a bad day and be a dick. Fight the automatic tendency to think it has something to do with you and hold space for his emotions to pass without internalizing it or making it a relationship issue. Maintain healthy boundaries and appropriate levels of respect for one another, but realize that not every bad day indicates that something is wrong with you or your relationship.

I know, I know. Easier said than done. But practice makes perfect, and it becomes infinitely easier when you remember to think in terms of primary emotions: fear, sadness, and shame.

Last but certainly not least, we started working on our vulnerability with one another. We had years of distrust and hurt to overcome, and it felt strange to acknowledge that we weren't really comfortable being vulnerable with one another.

Deep down, do you know that you have at least some walls built?

I'll admit that I'm guilty of this one.

I've always tended to be more logical than emotional and, to be honest, I took a great deal of pride in that. In my head, I equated being logical with strength and independence.

As the years ticked by in my life and my relationship became more confusing, more demanding, and less fulfilling, I continuously relied on that strength and my independent streak.

I found myself in the same scene, over and over: The day was done, dinner was eaten, kids were in bed, and there we were, sitting across the living room from one another, not speaking. Typically droning away to a TV show or mindlessly scrolling on a phone or laptop.

We didn't make eye contact.

We didn't talk to one another.

There had been one too many instances of the "same old fight." Eventually, I couldn't take it anymore. I felt like it was always my responsibility to bring him with me, get him on board, and force the conversation. Over time, I quit trying. I was exhausted. I gave up.

The tendency to put up walls became stronger.
I internalized the idea that I was just on my own.
No matter how much effort and love I put in, I was on my own.

Granted, this could have been an empowering thought if I had allowed myself to frame it that way. We are indeed responsible for our own happiness and well-being. To rely on others around us to provide that has the tendency to create unhealthy, co-dependent relationships.

However, I didn't see it as empowering at the time. Instead, I fortified all my walls.

I built them bigger. And stronger. More impenetrable.

My "I'm on my own" attitude didn't help our relationship, as you can probably imagine.

I focused on strength and stability. I stopped being generous, nurturing, and receptive.

The more my masculine energy increased, the more my husband's masculine energy increased to meet and exceed it. Before long, we were interacting with each other like two males fighting for the Alpha position. And that, ladies, and gentlemen, is not what you want in a relationship!

Two things that are very important to me and play a crucial role in my personal core values are honesty and strength. There are very few things that elicit an overwhelming emotional response in me; I stay pretty even-keel on a regular basis, and my husband has even teased me from time to time about that apparent lack of emotion.

Being lied to is the one thing that will set me off into another entire dimension of pissed off. I am furious when I know I've been lied to. Likewise, I do not handle hypocrisy well because hypocritical people are often living outside the realm of honesty. Whenever I see people saying that they believe one thing while behaving another way, I am quick to recognize the disconnect, put up walls of distance, and/or call attention to the hypocrisy.

Not surprisingly, over the course of 15 years or so, my husband has not only shown me hypocrisy, but he has lied to me as well. As our relationship moved more and more into the energy of two dudes talking shit to one another at the bar, my husband was guilty of some outright lies as well as lies of omission.

While I'm not a fan of dishonesty, I am a fan of forgiveness and reconciliation. The problem was, even when I attempted to forgive and move past whatever issue he had fudged the truth on, I never allowed myself to be vulnerable.

Over the course of our relationship, my responses to those situations typically did not come from a place of vulnerability and intimacy. Instead, I responded by building walls and closing myself off emotionally, all while telling myself I was practicing forgiveness.

I spent many years with those self-constructed walls in place because my husband had hurt me, and I was determined to never give him the power to do that again.

Did that work?

Absolutely not.

The walls I constructed between us only served to further that distance between us and magnify any problems that existed. And get this: He still hurt me over the course of the next decade.

That's because even people who love each other will eventually hurt each other, given enough time. It's just a fact of life. We can't control others, or how they behave, we can only control our reactions.

There will be times you inadvertently hurt someone you care for, or someone you care for will inadvertently hurt you.

The way to protect yourself against this unavoidable fact of life is not to put up barriers or emotional walls for protection. It feels good, and it makes sense in our deep, dark lizard brains to behave this way, but it is not a long-term winning strategy.

When you create self-imposed walls, you are creating an impenetrable fortress that, while it may block out some potential pain, also serves to block out all the good things that life can bring you.

Do you desire love? Money? Success? Health? Impact? The walls you put up block your ability to receive those gifts in abundance.

My friend Stacy Raske, leadership coach and best-selling author of *Be a Boss and Fire That B*tch: Quiet Your Inner Critic & Finally Believe You're GOOD ENOUGH,* explains that we naturally create these walls in the absence of healthy boundaries.

Instead of creating an impenetrable wall that keeps everything (good *and* bad) at bay, healthy boundaries serve as a fence, where you have the power to determine who and what comes into your yard.

The best boundary to put in place is to live with one rule: No disrespect.

However, Stacy points out that most teachings on boundaries frame the conversation in terms of interpersonal relationships when the most important person to instill this rule in is ourselves.

Until I stopped lying to myself and behaving like a hypocrite, I could not let my walls down with my partner.

Beauty can be achieved when you are fully vulnerable with someone you love. Many of us mistakenly believe that we are already vulnerable with our partners simply because we love them. But true vulnerability requires you to show up for yourself fully and authentically before you can show up for someone else.

If you feel as though you or your partner struggle with being vulnerable with one another, I would highly encourage you to look inward. Explore the ways in which you might be disrespecting yourself, whether it be in terms of your health, body, emotions, time, goals, or vision.

You must hold the standard with yourself before you can hold the standard with someone else.

CHAPTER SIX

A SHARED VISION

As the years passed and our lives became more complicated—bills, mortgages, business decisions, children—we continued to do life together. However, something about the way we were doing life just didn't feel right.

It was almost as though we were living side by side, both of us existing and operating in our respective zones. Of course, we had to come together to discuss some aspects of the shared life we were living, but there didn't seem to be an underlying thread weaving things together and helping me see the big picture.

It turns out that we had no shared vision.

To be fair, my husband had been active in mastermind groups, coaching, and personal development for years, so thinking about the big picture wasn't an area that he had entirely neglected.

He would even push me to set some goals or think about what I wanted the future to look like. But the constant struggle of life as Mom had me so deep in the weeds that I could not even see the trees, let alone the forest!

I felt bitter that he could see that bigger vision and set goals when I couldn't figure it out. I didn't know where to begin, but I felt like I was stuck riding his coattails and that I would, at best, be a secondary character in the life and times of Jeff Smith, watching his accomplishments unfold and seeing him achieve his goals from the wings.

Every seminar or mastermind meeting he attended resulted in setting big goals and visions for himself and our businesses but, to a much lesser extent, our family.

He would come home on that personal development high, full of excitement and motivation to crush his goals.

Part of me felt indignant and even downright mad that he was always the one who got to leave, fly to another city, sleep in a hotel, and interact with other adults. It seemed like a mini-vacation while here I was, unable to remember the last time I peed alone.

He also tightened his circles and was surrounded by other high achievers who were working on becoming the best versions of themselves, setting clear targets, and holding one another accountable.

But who was I surrounded by?

Unhappy housewives.

We were all a little irritable. We were all stressed out. We were all exasperated and feeling overwhelmed by life.

We were all so bogged down in the nonstop butt-wiping and mac-n-cheese making that it was difficult to even conceptualize what we wanted for ourselves.

When my husband occasionally shared his vision and goals with me and pushed me to set my own vision and goals, it never ended the way he hoped it would.

Everything felt like a lost cause to me.

Do I set financial goals? No. I don't even earn any money.

Do I set career goals? No. I raise kids for a living, and I don't even know what success looks like.

Do I set fitness goals? What's the point when I'll just be pregnant again before long?!

Every attempt to get me to set goals resulted in me re-hashing all the shit about my life that was disappointing or frustrating. I couldn't think about the future when I was so stuck in my present.

I was solely focused on keeping everyone alive every day; setting goals felt like an absolute luxury I just didn't have time for.

On top of all that, I was frustrated when he would casually approach me about goal-setting and act as though I should be able to rattle a few things off. To me, he had no appreciation for the shittiness of my life dealing with small kids day in and day out. He just didn't understand me.

My inability, or unwillingness, to set goals for myself was because I had allowed myself to stay stagnant and stop growing in my role. I stopped actively looking for ways to become better and expected growth or opportunities to just jump out at me or show up on my doorstep.

My frustration with myself and the state of my life was directed at my husband. I envied his time and ability to engage in personal development work. I envied the circles he was in.

I hated feeling like I was being left behind, both literally and figuratively.

He was growing and developing every day while I was withering away, an empty shell of my former self.

My story wouldn't allow me to grow: *There is no way to set meaningful goals within this life that I'm stuck in. I am powerless to guide the direction of my life. I have no control over money, time, or efforts—they all exist for my family.*

For many years, I relied on the visions that my husband would create to carry us through.

I wasn't bought in for several reasons.

One, I didn't fully trust him. I didn't know if he could get us to the point that he was envisioning. I wasn't seeing him perform consistently over an extended period of time and didn't feel comfortable putting down those walls and jumping in with both feet.

Two, it wasn't my vision. Sure, it included things that would benefit me and contribute to my sense of financial stability and overall quality of life, but it didn't speak to my *purpose*. It only served to highlight my disappointment with my life as a stay-at-home mom and the rudderless feeling that had me drifting through my days aimlessly.

Eventually, we realized that one vision wasn't enough. Thankfully, my husband didn't give up on me as that gap between us widened. He remained persistent when I struggled to speak the same language as him and embrace the woo-woo power of visualizing, goal setting, and reverse-engineering our lives.

As I began questioning more of my deeply held stories and challenging my own assumptions, I started to entertain the possibility that there was more out there available to me than I had previously thought.

We eventually settled on each writing our own vision. This took some effort on my part, and it was terrifying.

What if our visions didn't line up when we shared them?

What if he laughed at my vision?

Who was I to create a big, powerful vision anyway?

I sucked it up and leaned into the fear.

I wrote a vision and shared it with my husband as I took my turn to read his vision. Turns out, they were pretty damn close! We both saw ourselves spending time with our kids in nature, with true freedom of movement and time. Coincidentally, an RV appeared in both of our visions as well! There were some things in his vision unique to him and his calling in life, just as there were things in my vision unique to me.

This enabled us to put our visions together to create a road map that would guide our family. This not only served as the thread to connect us and tie in our separate efforts, but it did a great deal to increase trust.

There is something to be said for having the knowledge that your partner is working toward your shared goals and with your shared vision in mind. I was able to stop micromanaging and feeling like I needed to examine all the decisions he was making, and I was able to start trusting that he was making moves with our vision in mind even when I might not understand his actions.

Today, we have built on this exercise to ensure that we are always operating on our shared vision and setting intentional goals to help us move closer to realizing it.

Every year, between Thanksgiving and Christmas, we make it a priority to get away and complete year-end planning, just the two of us — no distractions.

We go over the previous year: What worked, what didn't, what are we happy about, what we achieved.

We revisit our visions and adjust the shared vision for our family as necessary.

We take the opportunity to set our goals for the upcoming year. From there, we set 90-day action items that break our goals into manageable chunks. Personally, I prefer to set goals in different aspects of my life: family, marriage, finances, fitness, personal development, etc.

We have undertaken this exercise for the past few years. I'm happy to report that every year, we have crushed the vast majority of our goals.

You may be in a place where you feel that gap widening between you and your husband. If that's the case, it is imperative that you get very clear on your desire to close that gap.

Many husbands are not looking at the big picture. They are investing in themselves, joining groups, and focusing on their personal development or business growth. They are continuously improving the quality of their social circles. They may be narrowly focused on their goals and vision, forgetting the importance of bringing you along on this journey.

But odds are, your husband is trying to reach you and close that gap. He's just doing it all wrong.

He might be asking you what your goals are while you're in the middle of cleaning up after dinner or searching for a kid's missing shoe. Sometimes our spouses mean well, and their intentions are great, but they're unable to read the room, or their timing is shit.

If your husband is leading from the front, setting goals, and working on them consistently, allow yourself to be vulnerable.

Let him know you want to grow with him, but you might not know how. That can be a tough thing to admit.

Let him know if you feel jealous or resentful that he gets time away to invest in himself and you feel stuck at home.

Let him know that it feels like he's growing, but it feels like you're shrinking.

Become aware of the people you surround yourself with and be intentional with the relationships in which you invest your time and energy. Model the positive behavior and growth that you see exemplified by your husband and be honest about where you feel stuck or frustrated.

If you feel like you're stuck living the life of an unhappy housewife, this is not just a problem for you. This is a big problem for your husband, too. Keep in mind that you might not be telling him how you feel, but we have a knack for picking up on the fact that our partners aren't happy. Individually, you must be clear on what you want in life and where you're headed.

This is not necessarily an easy task.

Before we could set our personal and shared visions, we had individual work to do. Past traumas can be a hindrance in your life long after you think they are resolved.

How are the experiences or subconscious lessons acquired from your family of origin affecting you today? How are the events in your marriage holding you back from the connection and growth you both seek?

There is never a downside to doing the internal work necessary to get clarity on who you are and what stories are holding you back from achieving your vision. While the payoff might be huge and lead you to change your stories or break through a glass ceiling, that doesn't mean it's easy. It's likely to be some of the most difficult but rewarding work you do in life.

Like my husband, I was carrying around plenty of baggage on a daily basis. I had a phenomenal childhood with loving parents, but I still had stories about money, financial risk, and trust that I needed to closely examine and come to terms with.

When we both committed to doing the *real* internal work, we were able to open doors to the best versions of ourselves. We utilized therapies like EMDR and Brainspotting, established core values (both personally and for our family), set goals, created vision boards, and listed our gratitude every morning and our wins every evening.

When you can cut through all the extra noise, you'll start to see where you want to go.

CHAPTER SEVEN

YOU ARE THE CEO

As a stay-at-home mom, my job was to take care of our house and kids, and a lot of the time, it seemed like I was sucking at both. I felt like I was living the old adage of half-assing multiple things when I needed to be whole-assing my efforts on one thing.

Because of the shared visioning I did with my husband, I continued working on mindset and thinking about how I was spending my time in very specific terms. Additionally, my older girls were at the age where they were awake all day and needing more meaningful interactions than I was able to provide when I was constantly distracted by endless housekeeping tasks.

While I had been home with these kids and these messes, I had also been involved in building a successful business with my husband, although I never gave myself credit for the work I was doing. I watched him transition roles over time. He developed from being self-employed and working *in* his business constantly to becoming a business owner and working *on* his business. Luckily, he was more adept at scaling and growth than I was, and the example he set provided a valuable lesson for me in how to become a CEO.

Attention: Ladies who are struggling with all your miscellaneous jobs and feeling underwater, I have news for you!

YOU are the CEO of your house.

Does a CEO scrub the toilets at her business? Odds are, she did back in the day before she had employees. You know, back when it was a start-up and a one-man-band. But eventually, it became necessary to outsource the work that didn't make her money to someone else so she could focus on more important, higher-value tasks.

As companies grow, the owner doesn't stay in the same role with the same responsibilities and continue to scrub those toilets. When Jeff Bezos started Amazon in his garage, he was the toilet scrubber. Fast forward 10 or 20 years, and he's no longer grabbing his cleaning caddy and hitting the warehouse bathrooms.

The reason for this is that his company grew, and his skills, time, and effort became more valuable elsewhere. Why spend your (very limited) time focusing on the $10/hour tasks when you still have $100/hour or $1,000/hour tasks that need to be done?

Model this in your house and create space for yourself to become happier, more present, and more fulfilled.

What are the low-value tasks that must get done? Make a list and figure out what can be outsourced for a relatively low cost.

Maybe it's a housekeeper once every week or two. Maybe it's someone who comes to fold laundry and put it away. Maybe it's as simple as switching from in-store grocery buying to curbside pickup.

Where can you leverage your money and other people to create time and space for yourself and your family?

The fact of the matter is, you were the one-man band, small business start-up years ago, back when you had that one baby who slept nonstop, and you had the time to sip Starbucks and stroll the aisles at Target.

Fast-forward 3, 5, maybe 10 years. Life might look very different now.

Maybe you've added another kid or two (or three), and now they. always. need. something.

Your role as a mom changes substantially as your children grow. Frazzled, sleep-deprived parents of babies and toddlers love to tell themselves that it gets easier. Sorry, no such luck.

Sure, some things get easier. The pressure to make sure your child doesn't choke on a Lego or drown in a swimming pool decreases with time. But it is replaced by other challenges like helping your children navigate interpersonal relationships, gain confidence in the areas where they may struggle, puberty, first crushes, and becoming good, upstanding citizens.

As you grow as a mother, your list of obligations and tasks will grow exponentially: The kids need snacks, they need meals, they need trips to the dentist, they need help with homework, they need more in-depth conversations when they ask endless questions about the "whys" of the world. They need more of you.

When you're in the midst of this chaotic life, it's difficult to envision what growth looks like. *How do I do the laundry or cook these meals better or more efficiently?* It's all just a bunch of shit that must get done all the time. And there never seems to be enough time. You take on more and more with no plans to outsource the extra work, only an expectation that you will do it all.

Momma: Your business has grown. You MUST grow, in turn.

There are a couple reasons to embrace this way of thinking.

First, at the risk of sounding like every sweet old lady at the grocery store who touches your arm and says wistfully, "Enjoy it. It goes by so fast," she ain't wrong. Your kids will NEVER look back on their childhood and say, "My mom was the best mom because she could really clean the hell outta that kitchen!"

They'll remember the time you spent playing outside, or with their doll-house, having a dance party, or just coloring at the kitchen table. Those are where the meaningful questions are asked, memories are made, and life lessons are taught.

Your husband might love having a nice dinner made for him when he comes home. But I bet you a dollar to a donut he'd trade that meal to see you less stressed over dishes and less resentful about how he's not showing up to help you.

Additionally, continuing to embrace the same "job" you had years ago, with all its included duties and responsibilities, keeps you stagnant.

Have you ever struggled with feeling somewhat disappointed in this life?

Have you asked yourself — like I did, "Is this really all there is?!"

Have you felt left behind as your husband grows, develops, or sets goals and you're sitting at home running through the same monotonous tasks day in and day out for years on end, realizing that you wouldn't even know where to start if you were to set goals for yourself?

Have you ever felt like having kids turned a once-witty, beautiful young woman into a frumpy troll with a brain-turned-mush that you don't even recognize anymore?

The reason all those things might sound familiar is because you stopped growing.

No one talks about the need for you to grow into your role as the CEO of your house and run it like a business. So most of us end up adding more and more to our plates, getting more and more exhausted or resentful, and then magically wind up an unhappy housewife.

This may seem like a simple concept as you read it, but many of us have stories in our minds that we accept as true, and that make putting this attitude into practice extremely challenging.

In hindsight, I realized that I had a couple of big stories tied to my unwillingness to offload the tasks I hated. They were very convincing little stories, and deeply ingrained, but they weren't serving me.

Story #1: *I will be worthless and have nothing to show for my life if I'm not stressed out about cleaning and taking care of the kids.*

It was a scary prospect to think about NOT having that impossible to-do list every day. What if a housekeeper came and did that shit? *What would I do? What would my job be? How would I show my accomplishments at home? What would success look like? Would I still feel like I was making my contribution?*

I defined my job as a stay-at-home mom as caring for the house and kids, so my husband was free to work, produce, and build a future for us.

I got so caught up in the details of what I thought a stay-at-home mom was supposed to be doing (i.e., cleaning, laundry, cooking) that I became too task-oriented and less goal-oriented.

I can manage the employees at my business (a.k.a. those who help with our house), or I can delegate things like the kids' ABCs to a Mother's Day

Out program and be more efficient, effective, and valuable as the support system that keeps my husband working, producing, and building. Limiting my own stress and busy-ness also allowed me to be more present with my kids and enjoy our time together.

Creating that time and space for myself allowed me to grow into a more productive wife and mom. I wasn't doing less when I outsourced those tasks; I ended up doing much more. And I did it better because I was leveling up personally to work for my family and focus on my highest-value tasks.

Story #2: *I have no right to ask my husband for the money he earns to pay someone else to do the tasks I willingly signed up for. If I have to pay for help, I am a failure.*

When I was still deep in the "cleaning the toilets is my job" way of thinking, I equated my completion of tedious household tasks with my husband's production of money.

There are some major financial hurdles to overcome as a stay-at-home mom because you technically don't have any of your own money. Even the most secure and generous financial arrangements or separate spending accounts are still subject to hesitation and guilt when it comes to spending money. This is especially true when it's for yourself or for something that could be deemed "frivolous."

My self-talk looked like this: *Jeff goes out and works hard for our money every single day. I'm supposed to have things under control here and take care of the house. How can I ask him to spend the money he's out there earning each day to pay someone else to do the things I'm supposed to be doing?*

Yes, it was technically *our* money, but it wasn't lost on me that he was the one bringing it home. Sure, my effort allowed him to bring it home, and there was certainly a value attached to that, but I still felt extremely insecure about the fact that I was never the one depositing the checks into the bank account.

To counter my self-imposed narrative, I had to embrace the notion of growth and actively work on my personal development as I transitioned into becoming the CEO of the house.

When you run a business, sometimes you invest back into that business to facilitate growth, automation, or more efficient processes.

I had to continue to conceptualize our household as a business, and I was tasked with ensuring its growth and success. By making investments back into the business of our household, our overall business grew and started to operate more efficiently and with happier employees.

If you're struggling to develop into the CEO of your house and still regard yourself like an unpaid housekeeper or nanny, make a list of the busy work you are responsible for.

Go over your list and make a note of the items that could be delegated to someone else.

Ask yourself (*really* ask yourself) how you feel about handing those tasks to someone else.

Will it make you anxious? Why?

Will it make you feel out of control? Why?

Does it feel like giving part of yourself away? Why?

Explore the stories that you might be holding on to that are prohibiting you from growing and running your house like the CEO.

Many of us get hung up on the financial implications of paying someone else to complete these tasks. It's important to remember that money is a tool, and it's certainly not a finite resource. Odds are, you can make more money.

Perhaps the amount you spend on childcare, housekeeping, or help with the laundry will carry a greater return on investment than you can imagine.

While you can create more income, you can never create more time.

Money is a tool to buy time. More time for yourself, more time with your children, and more time with your spouse.

CHAPTER EIGHT

WHY CAN'T I GET ANY TIME?

Life is hard when you're a mom of young kids during those "solitary confinement" years.

Your husband gets to leave the house every day for work and human interaction while you're stuck inside, with these kids who spend their days behaving like obnoxious, drunk midgets.

For me, the biggest reminder of this discrepancy in roles and freedom (or lack thereof) was our time for fitness.

My husband had the time to make fitness a priority for himself: He was lifting weights at the gym, going on long bike rides while listening to podcasts, or doing anything else that suited his fancy—or so it seemed to me. Meanwhile, I had my cheek pressed against the windowpane, longing for the outside world.

His fitness and routines were always a priority to him and, as such, they didn't get skipped. On the other hand, I couldn't count the number of times that I planned to go walking, go to the gym, or do something for myself and had life throw me a curveball.

Oh, a kid threw up and can't go to school today? That's fine. I'll just scrap my plans to work out.

Oh, the plumber is coming at 10:00 am? Well, I guess I'll skip the gym today. I mean, somebody has to be here to deal with that.

I began to feel as though I was constantly sacrificing and creating the space for my husband to prioritize what was important to him, but he was unwilling or unable to do the same for me.

This perception was fueled by my negative body image. My husband, a talented and natural athlete, has been in shape since the day I met him. When life gets hectic, and he isn't as diligent about making the time to work out, one session back in the gym is all it takes to be beach-body ready again. It's absolutely maddening.

Here I sat as a 20-pound fatter version of myself, not feeling good about my reflection when I got in and out of the shower, not fitting in any of my clothes, and certainly not feeling like a strong, sexy, or confident woman.

Why can't he create the space for me to get away and workout like I do for him?

Why do my priorities have to take a backseat to everyone else's?

These were the questions I asked myself frequently. Maybe not outright. But subconsciously, for sure.

The only explanation became my newest story: *My husband doesn't care about my goals.*

But here's the problem: if I had set a fitness goal (let's say I wanted to get back to a pre-baby weight), I certainly had *not* set a plan to help me achieve it or a timeline to accomplish it. Without a plan or a by-when, your goal is meaningless; it's just a someday dream. A lot of bark with no bite.

I never truly set a goal for myself. I just bitched and felt bad about my current reality.

Secondly, if my husband had created the time and space for me to get away, would I have used it to work out? Probably not!

Real talk: I told myself I would go work out, but when I got the time alone, I ended up getting a pedicure or grabbing a happy hour margarita with a girlfriend who I hadn't seen in a while (or maybe just by myself). Hell, many times I simply sat in my car and stared at my phone, disconnecting from all my responsibilities as a form of sedating and simply reveling in the peace and quiet.

I started to reinforce this new story in my mind, one that included a husband who could not and/or would not prioritize my goals. A husband who only cared about his own fitness plans and the things he was working to accomplish but didn't care about what I needed or wanted.

My tough realization was that my hurt and resentment that stemmed from my husband not prioritizing my health and fitness goals wasn't rooted in his lack of desire to support me.

It was firmly rooted in my lack of health and fitness goals, in my failure to prioritize my time for what I said mattered, and my expectation that I didn't need to say what I wanted or explain how I needed support.

I expected him to read my mind. To just automatically know how to be a team player on this (relatively) new team of a family we had. When to be perfectly honest, I didn't even know what I was doing half the time!

I expected my husband to prioritize things for me that I wasn't prioritizing for myself. In doing so, I was holding him to a standard that I was unwilling to hold myself to. Until I spoke up, set some goals, and behaved in a way that supported those goals, I had zero grounds to let those negative feelings manifest.

Perhaps you have been guilty of these actions and this mindset in the past?

Have you ever decided to take up a new way of eating? Perhaps you heard about someone who had great success with keto, so you figure, *why the hell not?! This is a keto house now! Watch out world – we're about to get fit AF! All carbs go straight into the trash can!*

And perhaps your husband has watched this scene play out before, like six months ago when a different diet was all the rage? So he gives you the old eye roll and a "Sure thing, honey," but he seems unwilling to turn his life upside-down to commit to this new way of life.

Next thing you know, he makes a grocery store run and comes home with more carbs! Now, naturally, you eat them because I mean…. they're here now, so you might as well. But why would he sabotage you like that? Clearly, your goals don't matter to him.

Sometimes, we don't take full responsibility for our goals or commitments, so we scapegoat our partners when we fail.

Your actions and lack of commitment are dictating the level of support you receive from the people around you.

I cannot overstate what a colossal discovery this was for me.

It took me years to come to this realization, but once I was willing to acknowledge that no one else was responsible for my health and fitness except me, my entire life changed.

Undoubtedly by now, you've gathered that I was telling myself some bullshit stories for a long time.

I told myself stories about my worth as a woman and mother: *If I use the money that my husband is earning for our family to do something like hire a housekeeper, that surely means I'm failing at my job!*

I told myself stories about my husband: *If he truly respected me and thought I was an equal partner, he would do these simple tasks that I've been asking for to make my life and job easier.*

I also had all the stories about myself, my body, and my time to work out and take care of myself: *I am eating healthy; why can't I lose this weight?*

One of my most persistent stories was: *I don't have any time!*

Maybe you're guilty of uttering that phrase repeatedly. When you're in charge of raising little humans, the job is all-consuming. It starts early in the morning and doesn't even really end once you finally get them in bed for the last time.

When someone is sick, your whole day is thrown for a loop. In a lot of ways, your time and productivity are completely held hostage by your children.

It is easy to tell yourself that you don't have any time. I can't tell you the number of times I complained, "I just can't find the time!"

But ask yourself: Are you being effective and efficient with your time, or are you just busy?

It's easy to be busy; we all have bills, kids, responsibilities, groceries, and more. However, look around at uber-successful people. Somehow, there are people with those same (if not more) kids, responsibilities, and obligations who are getting more accomplished each day.

Why is it that we don't have time to work out?

Why do we not have time to prepare healthy meals?

The answer is because we're expecting to *find* the time.

The more convinced we are that time is just laying around somewhere waiting to be discovered like that $20 bill in an old pair of jeans or a crusty Sour Patch Kid in the couch cushion, the less we think about *making* the time.

Let that sink in for a minute. We tend to tell ourselves that we just can't find the time to do something. But here's the secret: No one ever finds the time; you must make the time. To make the time, you must commit and do the work so it will happen.

Sometimes it's the little technological or societal advancements that can have the biggest impact.

For me, this was the introduction and widespread adoption of curbside grocery pickup. When my littles were in their Mother's Day Out program, I would often use that alone time to run errands for my family without the hassle of dealing with the kids. And as you know, it is infinitely easier to go grocery shopping solo as opposed to arguing with kids about how they swear they won't pick out all the Lucky Charms marshmallows, leaving the boring cereal behind, for the 1,000th time.

What I ended up doing was wasting two hours of my five precious kid-free hours by roaming the grocery store aisles and enjoying my peace and quiet!

I created time for myself by ordering my groceries online the night before. After drop-off, I hit the gym for an hour while someone else shopped my grocery list for me to pick up when I was finished.

I got my alone time and enjoyed some peace and quiet.

I was doing something good for me.

I was following through on promises I had been making to myself.

AND – I was still headed home with my car full of groceries.

Same amount of time. Much more accomplished.

I guarantee there are aspects of your life where you feel overwhelmed by the to-do lists and odd jobs. I also guarantee that you are spending more time than you should on small tasks that don't move the ball down the field in any meaningful way.

To see where you might be losing or wasting your valuable time, one exercise I suggest is a time study. From the time you get up in the morning to the time you go to sleep, record everything you do in 15-minute increments.

Did you spend 45 minutes scrolling Instagram or watching TikTok videos while a kid was napping? Okay — no judgment — but record that. Did dinner take you 75 minutes to prepare? Did you spend three hours folding laundry this week?

Record how you are spending your time for two weeks; sometimes, one week is enough to see where the holes and gaps are. From that point, the goal is to develop solutions for the time-sucking activities — especially those activities we despise.

Set blocks for designated scrolling windows with a timer, so you don't lose track of time while using social media. Use a weekend day to meal prep, so weeknight dinners go more quickly and smoothly. Hire someone to come in once a week or two to fold laundry for you; it might be surprisingly affordable.

I had to come to the realization that I always felt like I had no time because I wasn't being disciplined with my time.

I wasn't waking up at the same time each day, and I certainly wasn't waking up early enough to start my day with a calm, productive tone. Instead, I was snoozing my alarm, waking up with my kids, and constantly rushing to get everyone off for their day. That meant I barely had time to get myself ready, feed myself breakfast, or identify my high-value tasks for the day.

If you want more freedom in any aspect of life, you must cultivate more discipline. You have to choose between what is difficult now but easy later or easy now and difficult later. Creating that discipline inevitably brings you greater levels of freedom in the future.

It was easy for me to snooze and enjoy my cozy bed, but it was difficult to feel rushed, hectic, and like I never had the time to do anything I wanted throughout my day.

It was difficult to get out of bed earlier, but it made the rest of my day easier.

I began creating that discipline by time-blocking. Setting a rigid schedule seemed too unrealistic with small children and their daily swings and lack of predictability, so I created 2–3-hour time blocks each day, starting from the time I woke up to the time I went to bed.

As I became accustomed to scheduling my time and started focusing my energy on becoming more productive in my day, I began to schedule things in a particular order to ensure that everything fit as I needed it to.

Think of your schedule as a jar or bucket. You have lots of little, tiny gravel-sized rocks and sand to fill it with. However, you also have a few large rocks that need to go in, too. If you pour the small rocks and sand in first and allow it to fill the bottom two-thirds of the jar, you likely won't have room to fit in the bigger rocks. However, if you ensure the big rocks are in the jar first, you can pour the gravel and sand in last, allowing it to fill the gaps and ensuring everything fits.

We apply this same principle to our time: Your "big rocks" are the things that are most important to you. They move your life forward, and you need to get them done. These things also make life worth living and cannot be compromised.

My big rocks are early-morning deep work, time at the gym, device-free time with my kids, and weekly date night with my husband. My little rocks are things like phone calls, returning emails, running errands, or cleaning the kitchen.

I'll admit, it felt strange at first to set time with my kids and husband on my daily schedule and calendar! *Shouldn't those things happen automatically because those people are most important to me?*

One of my mentors is involved in many different businesses and travels for work regularly. However, he has "Legos with Henry" scheduled on his calendar, so he can always make sure, no matter how hectic his work schedule becomes, he doesn't lose sight of the reason he works so hard. It doesn't matter how crazy life might get; no one gets to schedule a meeting during Lego time. No "Cat's in the Cradle" vibes here.

Similarly, this same mentor schedules reminders into his calendar to send a love note to his wife. It's easy to look at this and write it off as being automatic and not genuine. But if you choose to see it from another angle, he's taking the time to acknowledge what is important to him and where he knows he needs to put his energy. It's also an acknowledgment that he's not perfect and can't do everything he wants to do in life without some processes and procedures in place to keep him focused and on track.

Before you scoff at the idea of scheduling time with your loved ones, ask yourself if you're showing up for them and being truly present right now. Odds are, it might be an area of your life where you could improve.

One of the hardest areas of opportunity to acknowledge, let alone improve on, is how we prioritize our time for *ourselves*.

If you are not consciously making the time to do what is necessary for your physical, mental, and emotional well-being, you are asking for trouble.

Some of you might be familiar with George S. Clason's 1926 book *The Richest Man in Babylon*. Nearly 100 years later, this book is still considered a classic of personal financial advice and wealth building.

While this is not a book on time management or productivity, I think there is a valuable parallel to make.

Clason uses a series of parables about an ancient Babylonian man who started life as a poor scribe. Thanks to the valuable financial lessons he acquired throughout his life, he eventually became the richest man in Babylon.

In his first lesson, he explains that if you make 10 gold coins and spend 10 gold coins, you'll never get ahead. This is the ancient Babylonian version of living paycheck to paycheck.

However, if you're serious about creating and growing wealth, Arkad argues that for every 10 gold coins you earn, you take one for yourself, leaving the remaining nine to spend. Over time, those single gold coins that get skimmed off the top will start to compound, and you can even put them to work to create investments and other income sources, but you start building that wealth by *paying yourself first*.

In his second lesson, he warns his students not to confuse necessary expenses with desires. Even as a wealthy man, he still has a plethora of desires that will never be gratified

Think about how many times this has illustrated itself in your own life.

If someone gets a raise, you buy something you had your eye on.

Get a better-paying job, get a bigger house.

Regardless of how far we may come financially, we always have wants and desires to gratify.

Right about now, you're probably wondering why I'm talking to you about ancient financial advice and gold coins. Bear with me, I'm going somewhere, I promise!

If you are guilty of saying "I don't have time" or "I can never seem to find the time," you are guilty of paying others first.

You might not be trying to divvy up your 10 gold coins, but you are divvying up 24 hours in a day.

This is why you're able to look around and see people who are raising a family, have successful careers, and still make time for their health or that occasional getaway with their spouse.

Those people are diligent about paying themselves first.

We talked earlier about my mistaken belief that the busier I was, the more productive I was.

I never go to bed at night, satisfied with a fully completed to-do list. There are never enough hours in the day to get to all the items we truly need (or want) to get to. However, when we are not clear on what is a necessary expenditure of time and what is simply a desire, we risk allowing that which matters most in life to give way to that which matters least.

I begin planning my day with the tasks that must be completed to nurture my health and relationships: Quality time with my children, my husband, and myself (usually in the form of alone time at the gym). With the remaining time, I set 3-5 high-value tasks to accomplish that day. These are not items like "get an oil change" or "pick up the dry cleaning." These are items that will carry a large return on investment for my family or our businesses.

The rest of the day is a catch-all for the various administrative garbage that might get completed or pushed off to the next day.

When you place the large rocks in the jar first, the non-negotiables that feed your overall well-being and relationships take precedence; that which matters most will stop being sacrificed to that which matters least.

Stop sacrificing your happiness and wellness to your endless to-do lists.

Pay yourself first.

CHAPTER NINE

WHERE DID MY OLD BODY GO?!

Real talk: these kids do a number on our bodies!

The amount of physical sacrifice and setback that we endure to bring a baby into this world is some next-level stuff.

Considering that my husband and I owned a gym, I felt an intense pressure to look the part of a gym owner and repeatedly told myself that I needed to bounce back quickly after that first baby was born.

It didn't go the way I hoped.

In my first pregnancy, I wholeheartedly bought into the old adage that I was eating for two. Every parenting book I read said to consume an extra 300 calories per day. The only problem was, I didn't exactly know what 300 calories a day looked like.

Most of the time, I gave into a pregnancy craving and had that cupcake or a Twix bar just thinking, n*o big deal, I need some extra calories anyway!*

Somehow, in the course of those nearly 10 months, I had convinced myself that the choices I was making were healthy and in my baby's best interest: I cut out my morning coffee because I didn't want to consume too much caffeine. But then the afternoon rolled around, and I swung by

Starbucks for a Grande hot chocolate. Gotta make sure I'm getting those 300 extra calories!

Excuse me, what?

Oh, it's okay—I cut out caffeine!

I made unhealthy choice after unhealthy choice and justified them as perfectly acceptable actions. I mean, after all, I was growing a little human! My body was supposed to change.

I gained the most weight with that pregnancy, somewhere in the ballpark of 50 pounds. After my daughter was born, once I was cleared to work out, I hit the gym regularly with my newborn sleeping away in her car seat next to me.

Holy smokes, it took work.

I felt like the process took forever and, to be honest, even when I lost most of the weight, I didn't feel or look like myself again. My skin felt flabby; I had obviously lost quite a bit of lean muscle mass, and I still struggled with pockets of body fat that just didn't seem to want to budge.

Again, I told myself there was a perfectly reasonable explanation for this. Yes, I was celebrating this baby's first birthday, but I was still nursing, so *that* must be why my body was clinging to this excess fat. It made perfect sense.

At this point, I ended up pregnant with baby #2 and started the process all over again.

Although this time, I wasn't starting from my baseline weight and with any of my previous confidence that went along with my pre-kids "toned" physique. As the weight crept on with this pregnancy and slooooooowly melted off afterward, you can imagine how my body image suffered.

The things I tried didn't seem to be working. I ate what I considered to be a relatively healthy diet, and I was constantly working my ass off in the gym or running, but it didn't make any difference!

I was primed for a brand-new story: *My body just won't ever feel or look the same after having kids.*

The harder I worked in the gym to get my old body back, and the little to no payoff I saw to go along with all my hard work, deprivation, and stress only served to reinforce that story.

I began to question my assumptions in 2017 when my husband invested in a one-on-one fitness and nutrition coach for me.

This was unlike anything I had tried before and, to be honest, I would not have spent that much money on something for myself in a million years! I think we're all clear that moms aren't exactly great at investing in themselves!

My coach was male. He was a powerlifter and fairly intimidating. Because we were working together virtually, I had to submit my initial progress pictures so he could monitor and assess how my prescribed exercise and diet were working.

I was several months postpartum, and we were just emerging from winter. Granted, a Houston winter is mild compared to where you might live, but we still stay mostly covered for several months. I remember the horror and embarrassment of having my husband take photos of me in booty shorts and a sports bra: stark white winter skin, the rolls, the flab, flesh everywhere. Mortifying. I felt like the Pillsbury Doughboy.

I sucked it up and went all-in with my new coach.

I learned about macronutrients and started eating a lot more protein than I was used to. My workouts moved from crazy intense CrossFit sessions to sets and repetitions of common barbell movements and some accessory resistance training. I wasn't soaked in sweat when I finished my workout, and I wasn't completely convinced it was going to be effective.

Nevertheless, I followed my trainer's instructions and trusted the process.

After a couple months, I started to see that flabby white skin tighten up a bit. Those doughy rolls started shrinking.

I also started to realize how much I didn't know.

It's okay to not know what you don't know. My expertise at the time was not in nutrition. I didn't really know what to eat, how much to eat, or when to eat.

That's the beauty of hiring a coach. He taught me the techniques I needed to learn to accomplish my goals, finally! It felt as though I had been fighting with one arm tied behind my back for years.

My way of doing things wasn't working; I would try one thing, get discouraged, then try the next thing and get discouraged. It was a never-ending cycle. I had already invested years into this process before hiring a coach.

I had been wandering around in the equivalent of a dark room hoping to stumble onto the magic formula all on my own.

Granted, I could have stuck with that not-so-winning strategy, but with the help of a coach, I accomplished goals in three months that I had been working on (and frustrated by) for three years!

I started working smarter, not harder.

Then, I came to my next awakening.

I realized how much I was lying to myself.

You've probably heard the phrases "Abs are made in the kitchen," or "You can't out-train a bad diet." I used to hate those expressions because I was fearful. I was afraid of what I might have to give up, afraid of not being able to stick with it and afraid of failure.

I associated more pain with shining a bright light on my food and how I was actually fueling my body than staying this slightly chubbier, post-children version of myself.

It was similar to how many people deal with debt. Sometimes it's easier to bury your head in the sand about what is going on or how bad the situation is, so that's exactly what we do. Let's just pretend it doesn't exist, shall we?

The debt doesn't go away. The problem doesn't get fixed. Odds are, the problem continues to grow because you're choosing to pretend it doesn't exist and avoiding the behaviors that are causing it.

That was my approach with food. I told myself that my overall diet was healthy, but I buried my head in the sand and chose not to think about all those pizza rolls I ate off my kids' Paw Patrol plates. I ever-so-conveniently forgot about all those handfuls of Goldfish or the 23 pieces of fun-size candy bars I stole from my kids' Halloween buckets.

I didn't want to think about, let alone be responsible for, the bottles of wine I was consuming on the regular.

I was tired, stressed, and never felt good about myself. I spent my days nurturing and caring for the people around me only to feel empty in the evenings and needing to be nurtured and cared for by someone else.

I found comfort in the food and the wine. It was a treat, a reward, a small hug that I could give myself to acknowledge the rough day, how bad I was feeling, and assure myself, *Everything will be okay.*

Emotional and stress eating is incredibly common for women, especially for moms. How many times have you thought to yourself, *I'll do that this evening after the kids are in bed?*

We tend to take care of others and their needs throughout the day, constantly pushing our own needs and desires to the backburner. We think we'll get to them, but how often is there actually something left over at the end of the day to give ourselves?

Never.

By the time the day is done, we want to curl up, disconnect, soothe ourselves with the wine and Goldfish Crackers, and fall asleep.

Not one of us has the motivation at the end of the day to *start* making good choices for ourselves. There is no 9:00 pm meal prepping or exercise session for most of us. Not consistently, at least. By that time, your motivation is drained, and just like your cell phone battery, it needs to recharge.

It took me some time to realize that I wasn't serving myself or my family by ignoring the issue and allowing this pattern to continue. I wasn't happy, I didn't feel good about myself, and what kind of example was I setting for my kids?

At the time I started working with a coach, my two oldest kids were around three and five years old.

Since they were girls, I was acutely aware of how we spoke to them about things like our bodies, food, and exercise. I decided to commit to examining the problems with my nutrition once I came to the realization that I didn't know the right way to fuel my body. And if I didn't know how to fuel my body, how in the hell would I ever be able to teach my daughters how to fuel their bodies in a healthy way?

That was the push I needed to clean things up and lead by example.

Kids have innate bullshit detectors. They know that mommy doesn't really believe you need your vegetables to be big and strong if you're skipping your veggies and popping pizza rolls and pinot noir after a stressful day.

More is caught than taught.

If you can't make the commitment to prioritize your health and wellness for yourself just yet, make the commitment for your kids and the lifelong (potentially even *lifesaving*) lessons you can give them.

I began utilizing tools to gradually improve my eating habits. I focused on the obvious bad behaviors: overeating, using food or alcohol as a band-aid, and my negative self-talk.

I focused on countering my negative self-talk with positive self-talk. After all, the stories we tend to believe are the ones we hear most often.

How likely are you to improve your health when you're constantly telling yourself that your body will never look like it did pre-kids?

How likely are you to examine how you're fueling your body when you keep insisting your diet is "pretty good"?

How likely are you to become the best and healthiest version of yourself when you've stopped treating yourself like someone worthy of good health?

I can never follow through.

I just can't stick with it.

No matter what I try, I can't lose the weight.

**Ask yourself if you would allow anyone else in your life
to speak to you the way you speak to yourself.
If the answer is no, then you need to change your self-talk, stat.**

It's okay to not believe it at first. But the more you counter your negative self-talk with positivity, the more you will start to believe it's possible.

I'm going to say something that might be unpopular in this age of body positivity: When you look good, you feel good. Period. There is no way around that fact.

When your clothes fit well, or when you feel confident wearing nothing but your skin, it puts a pep in your step that carries over to other aspects of your life.

While looking good and feeling good can be entirely subjective realities for different people, there has been a concerted effort in society and an active movement to make body shape and size a perfectly neutral observation with absolutely zero correlated health implications.

But – that's not exactly backed up by science.

Sure, beauty and health can come in many different body shapes and sizes, but excess fat, especially visceral fat, is directly associated with conditions like liver inflammation and insulin resistance. This means belly fat leads to poor liver function, and poor liver function leads to more belly fat. It becomes a tough cycle to break.

Do you know what else poor liver function and inflammation can do in your body? They can negatively affect your thyroid, impair the breakdown of insulin, disrupt your gut microbiome, and more!

There are strong correlations between excess visceral fat and the increased risks of heart disease, type 2 diabetes, and certain cancers.

Ignoring the side effects of packing your fat cells to capacity is not an act of love, whether it be directed at yourself or someone else.

This misguided self-love and acceptance is an implicit acknowledgment that someone who may be overweight, whether it be you or someone else, is incapable or unworthy of good health. I strongly disagree with this sentiment because I believe every woman is capable and worthy of enjoying good health.

We must be realistic about the downside and potential risks of not taking care of our bodies and allowing ourselves to slip into the comfort of poor health habits that are often disguised or even celebrated as body positivity.

A friend of mine spent a good portion of her life at a normal body weight. Over the years, as her weight crept up, she was embraced by other women and empowered by being "the fat friend," as she started calling herself. Just the other day, she opened up about her experiences and her realization that she had allowed this superficial version of self-love to overshadow real self-love. This led to a gradual failure to prioritize her overall health and well-being.

Here she was, struggling to get under 200 pounds, complaining about the cost and fit of plus-sized clothes, and listening to her doctor warn her that she was knocking on the door of diabetes due to the bad habits she had developed.

"When I look around, I rarely see old fat people. They're mostly gone by the time they get old, and I want to be an old person and be able to enjoy my life," she shared, in between tears.

In my case, not treating myself as someone worthy of good health had happened too slowly for me to realize it. I felt bad for gaining too much weight. Then I felt stupid for not knowing the secret formula to get the weight off. It started to affect me in a plethora of ways, as well.

Oftentimes, we kick the can down the road on tackling our body image or weight issues because we associate more pain with doing something than with *not* doing it.

It was easier to eat the way I was eating, go to the gym and do my regular thing, and tell myself that I was doing my best.

But I wasn't.

Deep down, I probably knew that, and it probably helped contribute to my plummeting self-confidence.

It's easier for my friend to find circles of women who will tell her she's beautiful and doesn't need to lose an ounce of excess body fat, but in reality, she knows she's playing a risky game of Russian roulette with her health.

Your health and wellness cannot take a backseat simply because you've decided to have children.

Each day, life presents us with an infinite number of choices. Starting from the time our alarm goes off in the morning, we get to decide between the hard thing and the easy thing: *Do I open my eyes and get out of bed, or do I hit the snooze?*

Do I go for a walk/hit the gym or find an excuse for why I can't get it done today?

Do I fill my grocery cart with nutrient-rich, whole foods, or do I grab the Oreos and Doritos?

Do I put my phone away and spend quality time with my loved ones or do I disconnect and keep scrolling?

These choices reflect immediate gratification and delayed gratification.

Does it feel better to roll over in your warm bed and go to sleep? Hell yes.

Even so-called early risers love the cozy call of their bed in the wee morning hours!

But think about those days when you wake up and get so much accomplished in your day. Or those days when you're ahead of things instead of running around in a haphazard way, reactive rather than proactive, feeling like your hair is on fire.

Rarely will you wake up early and think to yourself later that day, *I really wish I'd slept in a couple more hours.*

We acquire our health and fitness habits over the long-term in much the same way. We choose what feels good and gives us immediate gratification more and more frequently. Over time, these choices become our new habits, and it doesn't take long to see their effects.

If you struggle with body image or feeling good in your skin, know that you are not alone. We all struggle with this. Like I said, making babies is hard, physical, and very demanding work!

Begin by taking an unbiased observer's point of view: where are you choosing the easy over the hard? Where could you begin to train yourself to choose delayed gratification rather than immediate gratification? Where are you associating more pain with doing the work than NOT doing the work?

Is it more work to go to the gym and work out than take some time alone and veg out with a TV show or keep scrolling the interwebs? You bet.

Is it more work to purchase, prep, and eat healthy foods when we could easily grab takeout or microwave something after a long day? Yep.

Life presents us with daily opportunities to choose the option that is easier today but harder tomorrow or the option that is harder today but makes life much easier down the road.

Constantly choosing the former keeps you in a pattern of immediate gratification and giving in to the whims of your inner child. When the toddler inside all of us throws a fit in the evening because she wants sweets and we give in, we reinforce that behavior, just like we do with our real kids. Feeding that whiny little brat inside of us only serves to embolden her demands to get what she wants NOW.

The first step toward quieting that inner child is acknowledging that we live relatively easy and comfortable lives of abundance. There is no shortage of food or comfort; most of us have a freezer full of ready-made food and a warm bed.

Threats are relatively few; there is no saber-tooth tiger lurking around the corner to eat you or your babies. Human advancement is a beautiful thing, but we must constantly remind ourselves that comfortable lives lived unchecked will lead to complacency.

Imagine a great basketball team that spends its time playing against teams of a much lower caliber. Easy win after easy win eventually has an effect on the team as a whole. Perhaps practice becomes less demanding, standards slip, or players get distracted. Rather than continuing to improve, it's often natural that their skills will deteriorate, and they will begin to play just above the level of their opponents. When the time comes for the once-great team to play another great team, their atrophied skills are on full display to everyone watching.

When times are good and comfortable, it is a conscious choice to create the discipline necessary to build better habits. If left unchallenged, we will become softer, lazier, and more complacent.

It is an active choice to choose the healthy option over the convenient option. It is an active choice to make the time to work out rather than relax or fill your time with another activity. Those choices, while harder today, make your life easier down the road.

The easy choices lead to long-term consequences: unhappiness with our body image, a deteriorating sex life, and intimacy with our partners, that shitty feeling when you try on everything in your closet and realize that nothing really fits anymore, and you end up dressing to hide the parts of your body that make you feel self-conscious.

Even worse, these decisions can eventually bring you to a point of facing extreme health complications. It's only with brutal honesty and self-awareness that you can acknowledge hard truths. Continuously making the easy, comfortable choice eventually gets you to a hard, uncomfortable place.

The inverse is true: The healthier choices today compound over time, so you like what you see in the mirror. You feel good about your body, and you feel confident in the fact that you are someone who can do hard things. No one can take these accomplishments away from you.

Following through on what you tell yourself you want to do, or should do, creates an abundance of self-trust and self-confidence that cannot be replicated in other ways.

CHAPTER TEN

THAT LITTLE VOICE INSIDE

If you are a mother, you know the suffocating joy that is motherhood. You know, when you're at home with little kids, and they constantly touch you, need you, cry for you, want to be held by you, and come to the bathroom with you? That's what I'm talking about.

Let's be honest — if you're past that phase now and your kids are older, odds are they don't need you quite as much. Or, perhaps when they do need you, they're less likely to express it as openly as they did when they were that sweet-but-clingy toddler. While a part of us might miss those days of being needed so badly by our babies, let's be perfectly clear about one thing: That time is *hard*.

I've always been aware of the important role I play as a mother. I am guiding and teaching the next generation of people who will write laws, conduct surgeries, or create life-changing products. However, I had a deep internal struggle with my sense of purpose *outside* the four walls of my house.

I overcompensated in those early years by aiming for excellence like most first-time moms tend to do. When I wasn't sanitizing every surface in my home or enrolling my newborn in swim classes like many other moms I knew, I was focusing on momming at a high level and striving for extreme performance. It was what I was used to in the past, and it was where I felt comfortable. I needed to be at the top of the class.

I embraced cloth diapering. Was it more work? Hell yeah, but I was supposed to work and be the best. I made chef- and dietician-inspired baby food purees. Was it messy and inefficient? Hell yeah, but if I had been expected to feed my baby store-bought shelf-stable jars of food, I had to outperform.

My purpose felt deep, significant, and meaningful within my family, but I still had a nagging feeling that I wanted another type of purpose.

Occasionally, my husband and I would casually talk about the potential of me going to work once the kids were all in elementary school and my days were free. Maybe a part-time job of sorts, so I could still be there with them in the afternoons.

That didn't sound fulfilling in the slightest.

Not to mention, I would be 40 years old before my youngest of four children entered kindergarten. Who on earth wants to hire a woman who hasn't been in the workforce for the past 15 years?

I wanted purpose – I didn't want a part-time job at the mall.

At the risk of sounding selfish, I wanted more.

This desire for more led to what we might call a minor existential crisis that lasted for years…and maybe wasn't so minor, after all.

You can probably imagine the raging cognitive dissonance that I experienced as I slowly came to the realization that the stay-at-home mom life that I had imagined, planned for, and embraced simply wasn't going to cut it.

That life was something I had chosen for my family, but not necessarily for me. I chose it because it was what my parents had given me, and I had seen the benefits. Therefore, I wanted to give my children the same thing.

The ability to be home with my kids was important and meaningful, but I was acutely aware of the sacrifices I had made and continued to make to create that possibility. While those are certainly important factors, you cannot live every day for others, despite how much you might love them or want what is best for them.

Over time, I became like that entrepreneur who is consumed with their business, who can't create healthy boundaries on the evenings or weekends.

I became like the mom who lives for her kids and, once they leave the nest, realizes that she has zero interest in her husband. It turns out she hasn't spoken to him about anything other than the kids for the past two decades.

I allowed myself to become defined by being a mother to my kids. And, to a somewhat lesser extent, being a wife to my husband. If you took those two identities away, *who was I? What did that person want in life? What were her goals and priorities?*

I didn't know.

The first step to solving this problem was acknowledging that it existed.

Like many things in life that make us uncomfortable, I chose not to think about it.

Perhaps this feeling will go away? Work itself out? Change with some more time and emotional maturity?

Deep down, I hoped I would feel better and find more contentment in the life I was leading because I couldn't see a way out with any of the alternatives.

After creating lifelong expectations about the fulfillment and satisfaction I would feel as a stay-at-home mom, it was profoundly uncomfortable to acknowledge that it may not have been the right route for me. However, I still knew the traditional 9-to-5 working mom route wasn't right, either.

I was trapped between two choices that weren't speaking to that little voice inside me.

Where was my calling? Where was I supposed to make an impact? Because I could feel deep inside my bones that I was meant to do *something*. I just couldn't for the life of me figure out what it was or how I was supposed to make it happen, so it still fit within those societal paradigms.

I had to choose: Stay-at-home mom who feels oddly unfulfilled and guilty about it, or working mom who has to put the kids in daycare and feels oddly unfulfilled and guilty about it?

What an awesome choice.

If we moms know how to do anything, it's how to extract the guilt in any given situation.

So I stayed stuck. For years. I knew that voice was there, and it was trying to tell me something, but I could never really make out *what* it was trying to tell me.

In 2017, that voice became the tiniest bit clearer.

When my husband committed to investing a substantial amount of money to support my goals and hired a coach for me, I took the first steps necessary toward rediscovering and rebuilding my identity that had been lost for so many years.

The action he took shattered many of the stories I had been clinging to for years.

My husband only prioritized his goals, not mine. BUT my husband just invested thousands of dollars in a personal coach to help me reach my goals.

Holy shit. Both of these stories can't be true at the same time!

I had to pick one.

Every weekday, I started hitting the gym for an hour after I got the kids off to school/Mother's Day Out/the gym childcare center, depending on their ages. I wasn't going to goof off and do a couple of random movements and then call it good. For the first time, I was following a plan, and I knew what I was supposed to do each day when I walked through the door.

This block of time became a non-negotiable. It became my routine, and, by and large, it did not deviate.

There were days I felt unmotivated to work out, but I always went to the gym.

Some of those days, I sat on a chair and scrolled through Facebook or Instagram in silence, and it was just what I needed. However, most of those days, I would eventually think to myself, *Well…I'm already here. I might as well just do what I had planned.*

And just like that, my habit of going to the gym each morning for some much-needed alone time eventually helped me create some discipline.

My habits and routine were getting results. I lost the baby weight from baby #4 in record time because I was moving my body and eating a higher proportion of real, whole food than Goldfish, for once!

My body will never be the same after having kids. BUT with guidance on nutrition and a targeted workout plan, I'm seeing changes in my body that I haven't seen in years.

Again, I had to reassess and choose my story. They couldn't both be true.

The structure and discipline fitness required was the push I needed to rediscover who I was and what I wanted.

It reminded me how to start setting goals and targets again. It pushed me to take control of my time and start *making* some for myself again.

The reason it ended up changing the course of my life was that it forced me to examine my stories. I couldn't hold my conflicting stories to be true, and I was, as the kids say, shook.

What did this mean for my other stories? How many narratives was I carrying around all-day, every day, simply accepting as true and never questioning?

While I continued on my health and fitness journey, I started to work on myself in other ways. I examined the stories. I was honest about where I had not been showing up for myself and others. And I started taking 100% responsibility for where I was in life. I owned my own dissatisfaction rather than placing the blame on my husband for not showing up according to my expectations.

Before long, friends and neighbors started to reach out. Many already knew we owned a gym, but they had watched my personal transformation and wanted to know what my secret was.

Right about this time, the world kinda stopped.

March 2020.

Gyms (and almost everything else) closed.

It was only for 15 days, they assured us. (Although we all know how that worked out…)

More than ever, the women I knew needed an outlet for stress, anxiety, and their bad Covid-induced habits of takeout, to-go cocktails, and an increasingly sedentary lifestyle.

I started helping.

I set up a small Facebook group and posted daily workouts for my Facebook friends and neighborhood friends. I sprinkled in the occasional webinar on nutrition (I had become a certified nutritionist by this point) and ran some habit-based challenges from time to time.

I offered guidance when I could, and I felt a genuine sense of happiness seeing these women take charge of something in their life they'd previously felt was out of their control.

I was watching women grow and level up in life right in front of my eyes.

They were stepping into ownership of their lives in a way they had previously believed to be off-limits. Almost as if their stories had already been written, they were just going through the motions and acting them out each day.

I was helping these women step into their power, grab the pen, and say: "I think I'll write my own story, thankyouverymuch."

Eventually, my attempts to provide help and create a community turned into a full-fledged business! I started to feel the purpose and fulfillment I had been craving for years and, even better, it fit into my life. I didn't have to choose between being a working mom or a stay-at-home mom. I started choosing the best of both and creating the life I wanted to live.

With 10 years of experience as a gym owner and an unhappy housewife, I began to understand what so many coaches and fitness programs were lacking. I knew there was a group of women I could help, and I knew that no amount of diet and exercise would counteract the power of the stories that might be keeping them stuck or constantly pulling them back every time they made progress.

There are no words I can use to describe my pride when I see a woman change the stories she's used to telling herself. It creates a lightness, almost as if a physical burden has been removed from her shoulders.

I work with many women who are on substantial, long-term weight loss journeys to improve their health. Some of them have tried every option imaginable to no avail: Gastric sleeve, tummy tucks, or liposuction. Not to mention every fad, prescription, or influencer diet that makes the rounds.

Some have success with those methods, but usually only briefly.

Their stories always find a way back:

I'm the fat friend.

No matter what I try, nothing will work for me.

The diets and the plastic surgery never worked because they never changed their stories.

My job is to lead a trail of breadcrumbs to the real woman underneath those stories and lead her to a place where she can see that those very stories exist independently of her.

Our stories can be shed at any point if we just decide to stop telling them to ourselves and realize how powerful we are.

Simple, but not easy.

I am a firm believer that you are much more than an actress, passively acting out the scenes of your life that fate or some other hidden force has pre-determined for you. Every day when you wake up, you have the choice to act out the story as it unfolds; you can simply go through the motions, or become an active participant in your life.

What do you want your story to look like?

What is your hero's journey?

What lessons have you learned that you can share with your family, friends, or loved ones to help them?

My re-discovery of health and fitness allowed me to re-discover myself and change my story.

I was guilty of being the actress just going through the motions and acting out the script.

I felt as if I was a victim of circumstances and that the deck was stacked against me; I was powerless to effect change in any meaningful way. By focusing on what was my responsibility and truly within my control, I could clean up my internal house.

I changed the stories I was telling myself.

I decided not to be an unhappy housewife any longer.

Once I had my house in order, I was shocked to see things around me falling into place. My relationships improved, my health improved, my confidence improved, all of it. The changes I had made internally started to manifest externally.

For this reason, I specialize in working with busy moms. I know the struggle; I've lived the struggle. I understand the frustrations, and I remember how it felt to lose myself.

Fitness is the tool we use to invest in ourselves when we're only used to giving ourselves the bare minimum. It is my preferred route to help women realize their potential and empower them to take control and write their own stories.

You might not think so yet, but I'm sure your story will be an amazing one if you take the time and effort to write it. Your next chapter can be anything you want—hit 'em with a plot twist.

ACKNOWLEDGMENTS

This story is my journey and the lessons I have learned, but it wasn't a path I walked alone.

I want to thank my entire Apex family for their encouragement, leadership, and support. I owe each one of you a debt of gratitude for believing in me and encouraging me to tell my story from day one when my voice was still weak and shaky.

Mom and Dad: Thank you for a great childhood and for modeling exactly what I hoped to be for my own kids.

Niamh, Rowan, Gunnar, and Brehm: Thank you for teaching me about my strengths and weaknesses every single day. I am blessed to be your mom, and I love each one of you to the moon and back, infinity. Thank you for your patience on this journey and for always forgiving me when I make mistakes.

Kintsugi is a Japanese technique to repair broken items, such as pottery. Rather than gluing the pieces back together and aiming to camouflage the cracks, they are repaired with gold, which serves to make the piece stronger and even more beautiful with time.

Jeff: I'm grateful that we stopped trying to camouflage our cracks and embraced the beauty and opportunity for growth in our imperfections. Thank you for always going all-in with me. I would do it all over again in a heartbeat.

ABOUT THE AUTHOR

Kirstin Smith is an academic turned stay-at-home mother of four turned entrepreneur.

She is passionate about helping women create a life they love and inspiring them to take control of writing their own stories.

She lives in Houston, Texas but works virtually as a mindset, nutrition, and fitness coach to busy women across the country.

You can often find her in the gym or on an RV adventure with the whole family, including their Bouvier des Flandres pup, Poppy.

Connect with Kirstin on social media or through her website: www.KirstinSmith.com.

DISCLAIMER

This book contains information that is intended to help the readers be better-informed consumers of health products and programs. It is presented as general advice on health care. Always consult your doctor for your individual needs.

Before beginning any new exercise program, it is recommended that you seek medical advice from your personal physician.

This book is not intended to be a substitute for the medical advice of a licensed physician or healthcare provider. The reader should consult with their doctor in any matters relating to his/her health.

RESOURCES

For supplemental materials, visit
www.ConfessionsOfAnUnhappyHousewife.com.

Connect with Kirstin on Facebook and Instagram (@thekirstinsmith).

Access her free Facebook group at
www.Facebook.com/groups/HealthyMomsLiveWell for a community of
like-minded women working to become the best versions of themselves.

If you are interested in one-on-one or group coaching programs, visit
www.KirstinSmith.com.

Made in the USA
Middletown, DE
11 May 2022

65623767R00076